PHILIPPA PERRY is a psychotherapist and for the *Guardian*, the *Observer*, *Time Out* and *Healthy Living* magazine and has a column in *Psychologies* magazine. In 2010 she wrote the graphic novel *Couch Fiction*, in an attempt to demystify psychotherapy. She lives in London and Sussex with her husband, the artist Grayson Perry, and enjoys gardening, cooking, parties, walking, tweeting and watching telly.

THE SCHOOL OF LIFE is dedicated to exploring life's big questions: *How can we fulfil our potential? Can work be inspiring? Why does community matter? Can relationships last a lifetime?* We don't have all the answers, but we will direct you towards a variety of useful ideas – from philosophy to literature, psychology to the visual arts – that are guaranteed to stimulate, provoke, nourish and console.

By the same author:

Couch Fiction

How to
Stay Sane
Philippa Perry

MACMILLAN

First published 2012 by Macmillan
an imprint of Pan Macmillan, a division
of Macmillan Publishers Limited

Pan Macmillan
20 New Wharf Road, London N1 9RR
Basingstoke and Oxford
Associated companies throughout the world
www.panmacmillan.com

ISBN 978-1-4472-0230-1

9 8 7 6 5 4 3

A CIP catalogue record for this book is
available from the British Library.

Illustrations and cover design by
Marcia Mihotich
Text design and setting by seagulls.net
Printed and bound by CPI Group (UK) Ltd,
Croydon, CR0 4YY

Visit www.panmacmillan.com to read
more about all our books and to buy
them. You will also find features, author
interviews and news of any author events,
and you can sign up for e-newsletters so
that you're always first to hear about our
new releases.

Contents

For Mark Fairclough (Dad)

Introduction

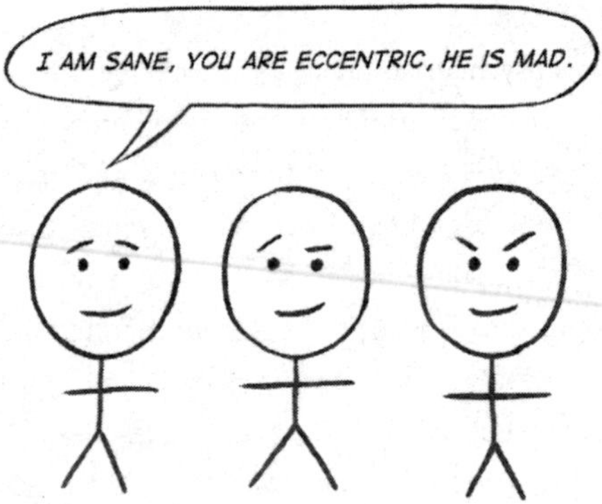
I AM SANE, YOU ARE ECCENTRIC, HE IS MAD.

In the *Diagnostic and Statistical Manual of Mental Disorders*, the handbook that most psychiatrists and many psychotherapists use to define the types and shades of insanity, you will find numerous personality disorders described. Despite this huge variety, and despite the proliferation of defined disorders in successive editions, these definitions fall into just two main groups.[1] In one group are the people who have strayed into chaos and whose lives lurch from crisis to crisis; in the other are those who have got themselves into a rut and operate from a limited set of outdated, rigid responses. Some of us manage to belong to both groups at once. So what is the solution to the problem of responding to the world in an over-rigid fashion, or being so affected by it that we exist in a continual state of chaos? I see it as a very broad path, with many forks and diversions, and no single 'right' way. From time to time we may stray too far to the over-rigid side, and feel stuck; few of us, on the other hand, will get through life without occasionally going too far to the other side, and experiencing ourselves as chaotic and out of control. This book is about how to stay on the path between those two extremes, how to remain stable and yet flexible, coherent and yet able to embrace complexity. In other words, this book is about How to Stay Sane.

I cannot pretend that there is a simple set of instructions that can guarantee sanity. Each of us is the product of a distinctive combination of genes, and has experienced a unique set of forma-tive relationships. For every one of us who needs to take the risk of being more open, there is another who needs to practise self-containment. For each person who needs to learn to trust more, there is another who needs to experiment with more discernment. What makes me happy might make you miserable; what I find useful you might find harmful. Specific instructions about how to think, feel and behave thus offer few answers. So instead I want to suggest a way of thinking about what goes on in our brains, how they have developed and continue to develop. I believe that if we can picture how our minds form, we will be better able to re-form the way we live. This practice of thinking about the brain has helped me and some of my clients to become more in charge of our lives; there is a chance, therefore, that it may resonate with you too.

Plato compares the soul to a chariot being pulled by two horses. The driver is Reason, one horse is Spirit, the other horse is Appetite. The metaphors we have used throughout the ages to think about the mind have more or less followed this model. My approach is just such another version, and is influenced by neuroscience in conjunc-tion with other therapeutic approaches.

Three Brains in One

In recent years, scientists have developed a new theory of the brain. They have begun to understand that it is not composed of one single structure but of three different structures, which, over time, come to operate together but yet remain distinct.

The first of these structures is the brain stem, sometimes referred to as the reptilian brain. It is operational at birth and is responsible for our reflexes and involuntary muscles, such as the heart. At certain moments, it can save our lives. When we absentmindedly step into the path of a bus, it is our brain stem that makes us jump back onto the pavement before we have had time to realize what is going on. It is the brain stem that makes us blink our eyes when fingers are flicked in front of them. The brain stem will not help you do Sudoku but at a basic, essential level, it keeps you alive, allows you to function and keeps you safe from many kinds of danger.

The other two structures of the brain are the mammalian, or right, brain and the neo-mammalian, or left, brain. Although they continue to develop throughout our lives, both of these structures do most of their developing in our first five years. An individual brain cell does not work on its own. It needs to link with other brain cells in order to function. Our brain develops by linking individual brain cells to make neural pathways. This linking happens as a result of interaction with others, so how our brain develops has more to do with our earliest relationships than with genetics; with nurture rather than nature.

This means that many of the differences between us can be explained by what regularly happened to us when we were very little. Our experiences actually shape our brain matter. To cite an extreme case from legend, if we do not have a relationship with another person in the first years of life but are nurtured by, say, a wolf instead, then our behavioural patterns will be more wolf-like than human.

In our first two years, the right brain is very active while the left is quiescent and shows less activity. However, in the following few years development switches; the right brain's development slows and

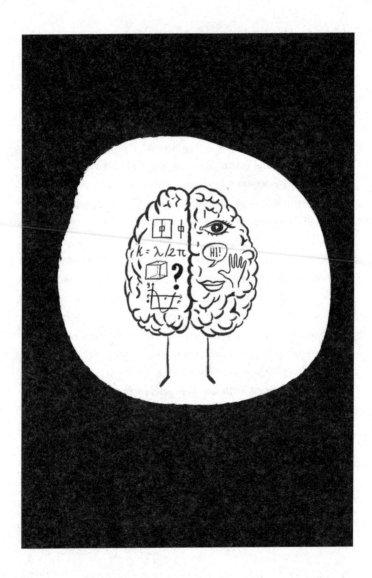

the left begins a period of remarkable activity. Our ways of bonding to others; how we trust; how comfortable we generally feel with ourselves; how quickly or slowly we can soothe ourselves after an upset have a firm foundation in the neural pathways laid down in the mammalian right brain in our early years. The right brain can therefore be thought of as the primary seat of most of our emotions and our instincts. It is the structure that in large part empathizes with, attunes to and relates to others. The right brain not only develops first, it also remains in charge. With one glance, one sniff, the right brain takes in and makes an assessment of any situation. As the Duke of Gloucester says in Shakespeare's *King Lear*, when he looks about him: 'I see it feelingly.'

What we call the left brain can be thought of as the primary language, logic and reasoning structure of our brain. We use our left brain for processing experience into language, to articulate our thoughts and ideas to ourselves and others and to carry out plans. Evidence-based science has been developed using the skills of the left brain, as have the sorting-and-ordering disciplines of taxonomy, philosophy and philology.

As I have said, in the first two years of life, left-brain development is much slower than in the right brain, which is why the foundations for our personalities are already laid down before the left brain, with its capacity for language and logic, has the ability to influence them. This could be why the right brain tends to remain dominant. You may be aware of the influence of both what I am calling the left and the right brains when you experience the familiar dilemma of having very good reasons to do the sensible thing, but find yourself doing the other thing all the same. The apparently sensible part of you (your left brain) has the language, but the other part (your right brain) often appears to have the power.

When we are babies our brains develop in relationship with our earliest caregivers. Whatever feelings and thought processes they give to us are mirrored, reacted to and laid down in our growing brains. When things go well, our parents and caregivers also mirror and validate our moods and mental states, acknowledging and responding to what we are feeling. So around about the time we are two, our brains will already have distinct and individual patterns. It is then that our left brains mature sufficiently to be able to understand language. This dual development enables us to integrate our two brains, to some extent. We become able to begin to use the left brain to put into language the feelings of the right.

However, if our caregivers ignore some of our moods, or knowingly or unknowingly punish us for them, we can have trouble later, because we will be less able to process these same feelings when they arise and less able to make sense of them with language.

So if our relationships with early caregivers were less than ideal, or we later experienced trauma so severe that it undid the security established in our infancy, we may find ourselves experiencing emotional difficulties later in life. But although it is too late to have a happier childhood, or avoid a trauma that has already happened, it is possible to change course.

Psychotherapists use the term 'introjection' to describe the unconscious incorporation of the characteristics of a person or culture into one's own psyche. We tend to introject the parenting we received and carry on where our earliest caregivers left off – so patterns of feeling, thinking, reacting and doing deepen and stick.

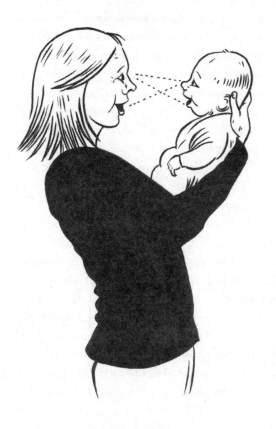

This may not be a bad thing: our parents may have done a good job. However, if we find ourselves depressed or otherwise dissatisfied, we may want to modify patterns in order to become saner and happier.

How do we do that? There is no foolproof prescription. If we are falling deeper into a rut, and/or deeper into chaos, we need to interrupt our fall – either with medication, or with a different set of behaviours: we may want a new focus in life; we may benefit from new ideas – or from something else entirely (I am being vague on purpose; what works for one person might not work for another).

However in every successful course of psychotherapy, I notice that change happens in four areas: 'self-observation', 'relating to others', 'stress' and 'personal narrative'.[2] These are areas that we can work on ourselves, outside psychotherapy. They will help maintain the flexibility we need for sanity and development, and it is to them that we are now going to turn.

1. Self-Observation

Socrates stated that 'The unexamined life is not worth living.' This is an extreme stance, but I do believe that the continuing development of a non-judgemental, self-observing part of ourselves is crucial for our wisdom and sanity. When we practise self-observation, we learn to stand outside ourselves, in order to experience, acknowledge and assess feelings, sensations and thoughts as they occur and as they determine our moods and behaviour. The development of this capacity allows us to be accepting and non-judgemental. It gives us space to decide how to act and is the part of us that listens to and brings together our emotions and logic. In order to maximize our sanity we need to develop self-observation to increase self-awareness. This is a job that is never finished.

2. Relating to Others

We all need safe, trusting, reliable, nourishing relationships. These might include a romantic relationship. Contrary to some people's belief, romance is not necessarily a prerequisite for happiness; but some of our relationships do need to be nurturing ones: a nurturing relationship might be with a therapist, a teacher, a lover, a friend, or our children – someone who not only listens but reads between the lines and perhaps even gently challenges us. We are formed in relationship, and we develop and change as a result of subsequent relationships.

3. Stress

The right kind of stress creates positive stimulation. It will push us to learn new things and to be creative, but it will not be so overwhelming that it tips us over into panic. Good stress causes new neural connections. It is what we need for personal development and growth.

4. What's the Story? (Personal Narrative)

If we get to know the stories we live by, we will be able to edit and change them if we need to. Because so much of our self is formed pre-verbally, the beliefs that guide us can be hidden from us. We may have beliefs that start with 'I'm the sort of person who . . .' or 'That's not me; I don't do that . . .' If we focus on such stories and see them from fresh angles, we can find new, more flexible ways of defining ourselves, others and everything around us.

Although the content of our lives and the methods we use to process that content will be different for all of us, these areas of our psyche are the cornerstones of our sanity. In the pages that follow I've examined these four key areas in more detail.

1. Self-Observation

When I advocate self-observation people sometimes assume that it's just another form of self-absorbed navel gazing. Self-observation is not *self-obsession*, however. On the contrary, it is a tool that enables us to become *less* self-absorbed, because it teaches us not to be taken over by obsessive thoughts and feelings. With self-observation we develop more internal clarity and can become more open to the emotional lives of those around us. This new receptiveness and understanding will greatly improve our lives and relationships.

Self-observation is an ancient practice and it has been called many different things. It was advocated by Buddha, Socrates, George Gurdjieff and Sigmund Freud among others. When we become practised self-observers we are less likely to trip ourselves up by acting out our hidden feelings, less likely to repeat self-sabotaging patterns and more likely to have compassion for ourselves and therefore for others.

The ability to observe and listen to feelings and bodily sensations is essential to staying sane. We need to be able to use our feelings but not be used by them. If we *are* our emotions, rather than an *observer* of them, we will veer into a chaotic state. If, on the other hand, we repress our feelings altogether, we can swing the other way, into rigidity. There is a difference between saying 'I am angry' and saying 'I feel angry'. The first statement is a description that appears closed. The second is an *acknowledgement* of a feeling, and does not define the whole self. In the same way that it is useful to be able to separate ourselves from our feelings, it is also necessary to be able to observe our thoughts. Then we can notice the different kinds of thoughts we have, and can examine them, rather than *be* them. This allows us to notice which thoughts work well for us, and whether any of our internal mind chatter is self-defeating.

To help explain the theory, let's look at this example: how a mother observes her infant in order to understand him or her. She mirrors back to the baby its expressions, its inner states and from what she observes she learns to understand its needs from moment to moment. Being observed, understood and met in this way is vital for the formation of our personality and, indeed, our survival. The practice of self-observation mirrors the way in which a mother observes and attunes to her baby. Self-observation is a method of re-parenting ourselves. When we self-observe it helps us to form and re-form.

It may help to think of our self-observing part as a distinct component of ourselves. It is self-accepting and non-judgemental. It acknowledges what is, not what should be, and does not assign values such as 'right' or 'wrong'. It notices emotions and thoughts but gives us space to decide how to act on them. It is the part of us that listens both to our emotions and our logic and is aware of sensory information.

To begin self-observing, ask yourself these questions:

What am I feeling now?
What am I thinking now?
What am I doing at this moment?
How am I breathing?

These simple questions are important because when we have answered them, we are in a better position to proceed to the next question:

What do I want for myself in this new moment?[3]

You may have made instantaneous changes just by reading the questions. For example, when we bring our attention to our breathing we become aware of how we are inhibiting it, and while we remain aware of it we tend to breathe more slowly. Change happens, if it needs to, when we become aware of what we are, not when we try to become what we are not.

I call these questions the 'Grounding Exercise'. If we do this, or something similar, at odd moments during the day and get into the habit of doing so, we can create a space for self-observation. Then if we are going off course we have the opportunity to re-direct ourselves.

When I did the Grounding Exercise myself yesterday, I noticed that, when I asked myself the questions, I felt dissatisfied. I found I was dreaming of replacing all my furniture. What was I doing? I was reading an interior-design magazine and I was breathing shallowly. After I had answered the first four questions I was in a better position to answer the last. What did I want for myself? What I wanted for myself, at that moment, was to exhale, put the magazine down and turn my attention to something different; and so I went for a swim to switch my focus.

Doing the Grounding Exercise helps us to place ourselves in our internal experience. People can be loosely put into two groups, those who *externally* reference and those who *internally* reference. Externally referenced people are more concerned with the impression they make on other people: *What do I look like? What does this look like?* Internally referenced people are more concerned with what something feels like: *Do I like the feel of this or that better?* Externally referenced people want to get it right for others (so they will be accepted, impress them or be envied by them) but internally referenced people want to get it right for themselves (so they feel comfortable with themselves).

I'm not saying that one way of self-referencing is always superior to the other but I do want to stress the desirability of increasing our awareness of how we reference ourselves, so that we can work out how we place ourselves on the internal–external scale. Too far on the externally referenced side and we lose a sense of ourselves and become off-balance. If, on the other hand, we swing too far the other way, towards internally referencing, we may find it necessary to adapt to society a little more, in order to be a part of it. We can ask ourselves whether the way we manage our emotions is prompted by what we imagine other people are thinking about us, or by what we know will make us feel comfortable.

Let's take an example: two people are sailing in identical boats. One is fantasizing, 'Look at me in my fabulous yacht; I bet everyone thinks I look cool and envies me', while the other is simply enjoying mastering the skill of sailing, feeling the breeze on his face and noticing the feelings that the open seas evoke in him. Two people doing the same thing but enjoying themselves in quite different ways. Many of us are a mixture of these two types; but if we often feel dissatisfied with life, it can be useful to understand how we are referencing ourselves; this in turn will allow us to experiment with change.

Internal or external referencing is one of the things to hold in mind while doing the Grounding Exercise. The Grounding Exercise is about finding out how we are functioning at any one moment. We can adapt the exercise for ourselves. For example, when I do the exercise I check how much tension I am holding in my shoulders, giving myself the opportunity to notice if I am tense, so I can loosen up if necessary.

When I am practising self-observation I also take time to notice what I call post-rationalization, which could also be called self-justification. This describes the way we have of mentally 'tidying up' what is going on inside and outside of ourselves, often coming up with convenient explanations which may be actually be nonsense, to justify our behaviour.

Experiments carried out by the neuropsychologist Roger Sperry have thrown into question the notion that we are rational beings led by our reason and intellect. In the 1960s, Sperry and his colleagues carried out some experiments on people who had had the connective tissue (called the corpus callosum) between the right and left hemispheres of their brain cut, in order to treat severe epilepsy. That meant the two sides of their brains could no longer connect or interact.

When the experimenters flashed the command 'WALK' into the visual field of the subject's right brain (bypassing the left brain completely) the subject got up and walked as directed. When asked why they walked, a question to which the left brain (responsible for language, reasons, labels and explanations) responded, they never said 'Because your sign told me to' or 'I don't know, I just felt an inexplicable urge to do so', which would have been the truth (as the action was triggered by their emotional right brains). Instead, they invariably said something like 'I wanted to get a drink of water' or 'I wanted to stretch my legs'. In other words, their rational left brain made sense of their action in a way that bore no relation to the real reason for it.

Considering this alongside further experiments that have been done on left-brain, right-brain splits[4] we have no reason to think that the patient's left hemisphere is behaving any differently from our own, as we make sense of the inclinations coming from our right brain. In other words, our 'reasons' for doing anything could be a *post*-rationalization, even when our corpus callosum has not been cut.

Even after our left brains have developed to give us the powers of language and logic, reasoning and mathematics, we continue to be ruled by the mammalian right brain. It turns out that we are unable to make any decision without our emotions. The neurologist Antonio Damasio had a patient called Elliot who, after an operation to remove a brain tumour, was unable to feel. His IQ remained excellent but he had no feelings even when shown terrible pictures of human suffering. We might think that, with his reasoning intact, Elliot could still decide where to go for lunch or what to invest his money in, but he was unable to make these decisions. He could imagine the probable outcomes of his choices, he could calmly weigh up the advantages and disadvantages, but he could not come to a decision. Damasio wrote up his findings about Elliot and other patients like him in his book *Descartes' Error: Emotion, Reason and the Human Brain*. This book concluded that, contrary to our expectations, a lack of emotion does not lead to logical, reasoned choices but to chaos. This is because we rely on feelings to navigate our way through our lives. This is true whether or not we are aware of our emotions.

In order to understand our motivation better, it can be helpful to spend more time with our feelings, which is where self-observation comes in. We will not be able to fathom all our feelings; and we should not cling to the reasons we so speedily come up with – some of these may only be a mechanism for self-soothing or justifying what the right brain has already decided upon. Instead we can increase our tolerance for uncertainty, nurture our curiosity and continue to learn. There is a danger when we prematurely reach a judgement about something that we stop ourselves from learning anything further about it. I do not advocate dithering about everyday decisions (such as what to have for lunch), but the re-examination of our beliefs and opinions from time to time is beneficial. As the psychoanalyst Peter Lomas suggested, 'Hold your beliefs lightly.' Certainty is not necessarily a friend of sanity, although it is often mistaken for it.

We live in a so-called 'age of reason', and yet, research such as Sperry's and Damasio's demonstrate, many of our ideas, feelings and actions come from the right brain, while the left brain makes up reasons for those ideas, feelings and actions retrospectively. Every war might only be the playing out of an old dispute that happened in the nursery, for which the leader concerned is still trying to find a resolution.[5] A lone gunman's killing spree results from a lack of empathy for others, more than from his particular ideology.[6] 'Ideology' is merely the reason he applies to his feelings – of, say, bitterness or hatred. When we argue vehemently against something, we do so not on account of the reasons we generate, but on account of the *feelings* that the reasons are created to support. They may be the 'wrong' reasons but our feeling is never the wrong feeling – our feelings just are. A feeling cannot be 'right' or 'wrong'. It is how we act out our feelings that is moral or immoral. A feeling on its own is no more right or wrong than a needle on a gauge, pointing to how much fuel you have in your tank. We might feel like annihilating someone but it is only the acting out of that feeling that is indicative of dubious morality.

A psychotherapist once told me when he was training that, previously, he had been sure that all his angry feelings were brought forth by the person in front of him, but as he learnt more about the psyche in general – and his in particular – he changed from pointing the finger and saying 'You, you, you'; instead the finger went round in a circle until he was pointing at himself, and saying far more quietly, 'Me, me, me'. As I have said, self-observation is the very opposite of self-indulgence. It makes self-responsibility possible.

Our post-rationalizing capacity – or what I am calling the left brain – means that we may come up with reasons not to self-examine. So if you decide to skip the self-observation exercises in this book, try to be more interested in the feelings that dictate that behaviour than in the reasons you apply to those feelings. You are being 'run' by those feelings, so rather than brush them off with your left brain, spend some time exploring them.

A psychotherapist is practised in hunting down the feelings behind justifications and fixed patterns of behaving and helping his or her client to see them. If you have the inclination and means, I recommend psychotherapy or psychoanalysis as a way of discovering more about the unconscious and how we integrate the unconscious with our logical side. However, it can be difficult to find the right therapist, and therapy tends to cost a good deal. There are other means and exercises that can help us develop the art of self-observation. There

words for how I
layer I can feel, they tak
ach other and to me, I can be thi
f having a bath and then I'm
emembering primary school. And yet
also keeping a list in my head of the
day and sort of sticking to it. Wh
I woke up this morning I was sti
dreaming after I woke up and
me a few seconds to w
as dream and what

isn't a right way to practise self-observation because one size does not fit all. I am an advocate of using whatever works. But however we get there, I believe that being able to self-observe is an essential part of staying sane. As well as using a focused attention technique like the Grounding Exercise, regularly keeping a journal can be a useful tool to aid self-observation.

A study in which half the participants kept a diary and half did not demonstrated the positive effects of writing something down about yourself each day. Diarists reported better moods and fewer moments of distress than non-diarists. Those, in the same study, who kept a journal following trauma or bereavement also reported fewer flashbacks, nightmares and unexpected difficult memories. Writing can itself be an act of emotional processing so it can help in many situations of danger, extremity and loss of control. People who keep diaries are admitted to hospital less often and spend fewer days there than those who do not. Research shows that liver function and blood pressure are improved in diarists. All personality types are shown to benefit from keeping a diary. I am particularly fascinated by the way that diary-keeping has been shown to positively affect several aspects of the immune system – including T-cell growth[7] and certain antibody responses. Studies have also shown that people who regularly keep daily 'gratitude' diaries, in which they list things for which they are grateful, report increased satisfaction with their lives and relationships.[8] However, these benefits are not the main reasons I recommend diary-keeping. I'm keen on it because it is a useful tool for developing self-observation.

A few hints for starting a diary: be honest and keep it simple; it is just for you. Try not to start with a flourish and then tail off after a few days: persevere! What you write is up to you. I am a fan of random memories, as well as what you are thinking and feeling at the moment of writing. I also like dreams. Dreams fascinate therapists because they dramatize experiences and parts of our psyches that we may not have processed into language. I recommend writing down your dreams and your reactions to them in your diary.

If you cannot think what to write just keep writing to see what emerges. In fact, stream-of-consciousness writing, done first thing in the morning just after waking, has been found to be effective in raising self-awareness. Write in longhand, and record anything and everything that comes into your head for a couple of sheets of paper.[9]

If you read your diary back to yourself you may identify some of your behavioural and emotional habits. For example, can you spot how much justification or reasoning you are using, or how much compassion you show yourself, or how much of what you write is fantasy?

Whatever method you find works best, keeping a diary is a way of processing your feelings, and getting to know yourself better.

Learning and practising focused attention is a key tool in the development of self-observation. Focused attention improves our ability to observe and experience body and mind in the present and without criticism. There are many names for this practice: prayer, meditation, contemplative practice and self-directed neuroplasticity. Learning to focus our attention is also a key part of the practice of mindfulness. This focusing of the individual's attention is a feature of many cultures and religions. Rituals as apparently different as Christian prayer and Sufi whirling are both forms of focused attention, but we can practise it whether we believe in a god or not. Practising focused attention boosts our concentration, helps with stress, anxiety, depression and addictive behaviours, and can even have a positive effect on physical problems like hypertension, heart disease and chronic pain.[10]

The practice of focused attention has further benefits. Studies have shown that the brains of those who regularly meditate or practise similar behaviours show permanent, beneficial changes. New neural pathways and connections proliferate. The pre-frontal cortex, which is the part of the brain associated with concentration, measurably thickens. The insula, the part of the brain that tracks the interior state of the body, as well as the emotional states of other people, also grows. Thus the practice of focusing attention for the purpose of self-observation literally strengthens and grows the brain. That in turn makes us more self-aware and thus better able to soothe ourselves, and it also means that we are able to empathize better with others. Practising self-observation helps to keep our brains flexible. Using it, we can become more aware of mental processes, without being taken over by those processes. It allows us to develop emotional resilience without repressing or denying our feelings. You'll find some exercises for promoting focused attention and self-observation in the exercise section in the back of this book.

One of the things we become more aware of when we develop self-observation is what I call 'toxic chatter'. Our heads are always full of chatter, littered with phrases, images, repeated messages, running commentaries on our actions and thoughts. Much may be harmless, but some can be toxic: hateful thoughts about ourselves or others; unconstructive self-scoldings; pointless pessimism. These types of thoughts can go round in circles; they get us nowhere and can cause depression. Self-observation allows us to impartially notice our mind-chatter and distance ourselves from that which is toxic. In this way the neural pathways that promote toxicity will be used less and will gradually shrink, while those that promote awareness and empathy will grow.

Using self-observation we can give ourselves the same sort of close attention that good parents give their children. As we saw earlier, such mirroring is the way children learn who they are and how to acknowledge, soothe and regulate themselves. Throughout our lives we have a desire and a need to be acknowledged and understood. Although this is most productively achieved in conjunction with another person, contemplative practice is one way we can achieve this on our own.

There is no limit to the number of ways we can develop self-observation. We may choose one-to-one therapy with a psychotherapist, analyst or other practitioner, or join a therapy or yoga group. One of my biggest increases in self-awareness came when I trained for and completed the London Marathon. Using focused attention techniques such as meditating whilst running as part of a transformative physical project, I improved my concentration, self-confidence and self-awareness more than I could have imagined when I began training a year before the event.

In conclusion, practising self-observation can give us more insight into the emotions that play such a large part in our behaviour. When we become more sensitive towards ourselves and more knowledgeable about our own feelings, we are more able to attune to, and empathize with, the feelings of other people. In short, self-awareness improves our relationships. Relationships are the second cornerstone of our sanity, and we will now look at their role and importance.

2. Relating to Others

A brain, like a neuron, is not much use on its own. Our brains need other brains – or, as we more often put it, people need people. We may think of ourselves as an 'I', and the notion of the isolated self takes up a lot of space in Western civilization, but we are in fact creatures of the group, like starlings in a flock that appears as one body against the sky, with each bird affecting and being affected by the movements of the birds closest to it. Our brains are linked together and grow together in relationship with each other.

We understand that the quality of the formative relationships we had as infants determines our initial place in the spectrum of mental health. However, it is also known that other people continue to be our best resource for staying sane. Any mutually impactful, mutually open relationship can reactivate neuroplastic processes[11] and actually change the structure of the brain at any stage of our lives.

I have seen such changes time and time again in many years of practice as a psychotherapist. I have witnessed clients become more fully themselves, more at ease and less neurotic. I believe that it is the *relationship* with the therapist, as much as any brilliant intervention, that brings these changes about. I learnt from Irvin Yalom, an American psychiatrist, that as a therapist you need to assess how clients feel about the therapeutic relationship, and ask them what was useful and what did not work in each session. As a young therapist I was often surprised that it was not new insight that was the most powerful catalyst for change, but the moment when the client saw that they had moved me; or when they felt accepted because I patted their arm; or when they saw that, even if I did not say anything at that point, I understood. But that is only half of it. I was changed by my clients too: they helped me to grow. In a relationship in which we are ourselves without a social mask and fully present, our brains are continually shaped. Seeing the world from another's viewpoint as well as our own can allow us both to expand. If we get too 'set in our ways', we are less able to be touched, moved or enlightened by another and we lose vitality. And we need to allow ourselves to be open to the impact of the other if we are to impact upon them.

Dialogue

The philosopher Martin Buber said, 'All real living is meeting.' He realized that only in relationships can we fully open ourselves to the world and to each other. Buber wrote that 'genuine dialogue', whether spoken or silent, occurs only when each of the participants really has in mind the other or others, in their 'present and particular being and turns to them with the intention of establishing a living mutual relation between himself and them'. I would add that in order to meaningfully connect to another person, one has to be open. This means being not who we *think* we should be, but allowing ourselves to be who we really *are*. This usually involves risking feeling vulnerable. Being open, and therefore vulnerable, does not guarantee that we will connect

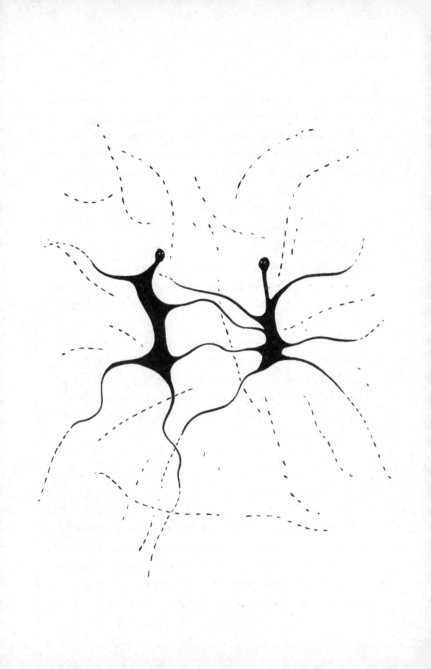

with the other, but if we do not allow ourselves to feel vulnerable, we deny ourselves the opportunity to experience genuine dialogue.

Buber also describes two other ways of being with others. First is 'technical dialogue', which is prompted solely by the need for objective understanding. For example:

'What sort of batteries do I need for this?'
'You need size AAA batteries.'

Second, 'monologue disguised as dialogue', in which two people who think they are having a conversation are actually talking to themselves. Jane Austen captured this process brilliantly in *Northanger Abbey*:

[Mrs. Allen was] never satisfied with the day unless she spent the chief of it by the side of Mrs. Thorpe, in what they called conversation, but in which there was scarcely ever any exchange of opinion, and not often any resemblance of subject, for Mrs. Thorpe talked chiefly of her children, and Mrs. Allen of her gowns.

Mentalization

The psychoanalyst Peter Fonagy coined the word 'mentalization'. This means the ability to understand our inner experience, and from that, work out accurately the other person's feelings. This process gives us the ability to make and sustain healthy relationships. If all goes well, we have early caregivers who carry out this process of mentalization naturally, and we pick it up unconsciously from them. This process is aided by self-observation, because as we develop and become more sensitive to our own feelings we also become more sensitive to what other people are feeling. This does not mean projecting our own thoughts onto them, but understanding, on the level of feeling, that the way they feel and think might be different from the way we do.

If we find people so unpredictable that we are unable to relate to anyone, then it is probable that it is the process of mentalization that is letting us down. There is so much that is unspoken and unconscious in the process of relating to another that the only way to learn it is in relationship with someone else. If our earliest caregiver was unable to provide a model for mentalization we will not have learnt it from them. But the brain is plastic. We can learn it later in life with a psychotherapist or in other close relationships. When we begin to understand what it really feels like to be deeply understood, we can begin to understand others and have satisfying relationships.

When psychotherapy began it was about the practitioner listening to a patient and interpreting what the patient said, in order to afford the patient insights about his or her psyche. But now we understand that the main curative part of psychotherapy is the relationship itself. It appears not to be relevant whether the practitioner is an analytic Freudian or a counselling Rogerian[12], a transactional analyst or a life coach, or from an eclectic school. What matters is the quality of the relationship and the practitioner's belief in what he or she is offering. In the same way, our sanity and our happiness will have more to do with our interpersonal relationships than with what the weather is like, or what job we do, or our hobbies. We run about, earning a living, achieving things and making a decent show of it all (or not), but what affects us most are the people around us: our parents, our children, our lovers, our colleagues, our neighbours and our friends. As the psychotherapist Louis Cozolino says, 'From birth until death, each of us needs others who seek us out, show interest in discovering who we are and help us feel safe.' A trauma consultant puts it more starkly, 'Everyone should walk through an Emergency Room at least once in their life. Because it makes you realize what your priorities are. It's not the rush, rush, rush and the money, money, money; it's the people you love and the fact that one minute they might be there and one minute they might be gone.'[13]

Staying connected with others is a vital – the vital – part of staying sane.

How to Have Good Relationships

This is a 'how-to' book and at this point I wish it was not, because as soon as we start to legislate for how to have relationships, we are already in danger of getting it wrong. This is because if we attempt to manipulate a relationship, there is a danger of treating the other as an 'it' rather than as an equal; of seeing him or her as an object to be steered rather than another subject to meet. Nor can we have a simple rule: 'be empathetic' – since empathy is only part of a process, not a rigid set of behaviours.

My friend Astrid had a rule she applied to relationships. When she was working out how she felt about someone she would say, for instance, '. . . And he asked me no questions about myself at all' – as

if she was seeking to prove something; but as I come from a different background I was not sure what it was she was trying to tell me. She explained that in her originating culture it was polite to ask questions when you meet a new person. If the other person does not return the compliment by showing curiosity in return then the suspicion is that they are self-absorbed and selfish. I thought that, as well as sounding like a post-rationalization for Astrid's not taking to a particular person, this way of looking at the world did not take into account the 'negative politeness' rule[14] which is an unspoken part of the rituals of my culture. Gross generalization coming up. Basically there are two sorts of cultures. In crowded countries such as Japan and Britain we tend to have 'negative-politeness'. This means that people are aware of others' need for privacy, and their desire not to be intruded upon. In countries where there is more space, like the USA, people are more inclined to practise 'positive politeness', where the emphasis is on inclusion and openness. The anthropologist Kate Fox says that what looks like stand-offishness in a negative-politeness culture is really a sort of consideration for people's privacy. So you see, for every overarching rule about how to have relationships, there will always be another that contradicts it. You may *act* in a caring way towards somebody, but if you have not absorbed the rules of that person's family of origin or culture you can still get it wrong.

Our codes about manners differ from family to family and culture to culture. Manners are a societal attempt to regulate the way we treat one another. If we follow manners strictly, we may turn into a 'supercharmer', and other people may doubt our sincerity. If we become extra sincere, we may appear over-earnest in a way that might be acceptable in, say, America but not in Britain. It is difficult to formulate guidelines about other people's feelings because they vary so much, from culture to culture, from family to family, from person to person, and from moment to moment. We are either good at picking up on people's feelings and attuning to them, or we are not. The way to learn how to be with someone is by being with them; if we cannot get that far we are a bit stuck. In trying to please one group of people we can end up offending another. Asking people what we are doing wrong will either upset us (when we get the answer), or will only tell us what we are doing wrong *in their eyes* – and it might not be us who is 'wrong' anyway. Adhering to strict guidelines about how to behave around others is a form of rigidity. Not being mindful of your impact upon others is a form of chaos. What we are seeking is a middle way, which can be defined as 'flexibility'; this allows us to reach out and respond to others with attunement. This flexibility is something we can aim for but we should not expect to achieve it in every encounter. However, if we find forming any relationship at all difficult, we may need to invest in consulting a relationship expert, a psychotherapist or another kind of mental-health worker.

Very often we begin a relationship or an encounter with another person by engaging in small talk about the weather, or by playing out the sort of rituals that the transactional analyst Eric Berne identified in the Sixties as 'games'. In developed countries, for instance, men may play a competitive game by arguing about whose car is best – 'You've got the X5 M? Oh dear, not enough power. You have to have the X6 M model like mine.' Women in such cultures, on the other hand, often practise competitive self-deprecation – 'You say you like this dress? But it's so old; I got it from a charity shop ten years ago.' That game might be called the 'Mine is Smaller than Yours' game.

For me, small talk and 'games' like these can, at times, feel far more appropriate than 'big talk', especially before I have formed a bond with the other person. I once attended a counselling course in which students were encouraged to abandon their comfortable rituals and games and express the feelings that lay underneath them. I found this hard, because I am uncomfortable with the type of 'real' talk that involves saying things like, 'I notice I am experiencing feelings of envy toward you' before I have even taken off my coat. However, some people prefer this way of relating to preliminary chit-chat. I remember saying to some of my fellow students, 'Does anyone want a coffee?' They all shook their heads and asked me to rephrase my question to reflect my real feelings. So I had to feel and think and then I came up with, 'I want coffee and I want you to come with me.' Having tried it, I found I really liked this process of turning a ritualized question into a statement, and I still try to do this when I remember. Although it is more of a risk (making a statement about myself rather than asking a question of another makes me feel more vulnerable), I find expressing an invitation like this gives me more of a chance of connecting to others. However, saying 'I want a coffee and I want you to come with me' with the old crowd of ex-students has become so ritualized that it is now no different to saying 'Does anyone want a coffee?' If you try to bring meaning to every single word it becomes exhausting (for me, anyway) and if the once meaningful utterance gets repeated it too becomes like ritual, just as those exchanges about the weather have become ritualized. Being real and open is a way to make real connections with others, but connections are made in more ways than simply exchanging meaningful words, and I would never rule out the significance of small talk. We need it in order to bond, and to pave the way for 'big talk'. It is the equivalent of monkey grooming[15] or the mutual sniffing that dogs do, and we need it. (I would not actually fancy doing what dogs do, nor do I want to look for your fleas, so I will continue to find out what you think of this weather we've been having . . .)

In *Watching the English*, the anthropologist Kate Fox has observed that rules exist about how to talk about the weather, and as this is a how-to book, I will share one with you. The point is that when I tell you we have had a lot of rain recently, what I am really wondering is not whether you know how many inches of rainfall we have had but whether you are an agreeable sort of person. I am more likely to form a favourable opinion of you if you agree with me. This is the rule of reciprocity. Remarks about the weather are phrased as questions not because we care about the weather but because we want a response. You may not be particularly interested in the weather but that does not mean you do not care about your relationship with the person you are talking to. It does not matter that the words we use for this 'nice-day-isn't-it?' ritual are empty. Such exchanges are not about what we say but how we acknowledge each other as we say it.

Unfortunately, whether we are adept at following such rules or not, we often trip ourselves up on the way to forming relationships, and sometimes stop ourselves from having them at all. There are many ingenious ways in which we unwittingly limit our contact with others and thus deprive ourselves of their potentially beneficial influence on us. Sometimes we assume we are having a relationship with another person when that relationship in fact exists mostly in our heads, because we are unknowingly misreading that person. Misreading can happen in several different ways:

- We can project ourselves onto the other person, so instead of having an 'I–You' relationship, we have an 'I–I' relationship; 'She will respond just as I would respond.'
- We can objectify the other person and have an 'I–It' relationship: 'If I phrase it like this, she will think of me like that.'
- We can also blur the boundaries between the person with us in the present with people we have known before, and transfer our experience of people from the past onto this person in the present, and have 'I–Ghost' relationships: 'If I do this, other people always respond like that.'

We tend to trust people in ways that are derived from past conditioning and experience. For example, we will have beliefs about how trustworthy a person is. Some people learn to trust no one, and this causes them to lead lonely and often isolated lives that restrict the possibility of full mental health. In contrast, there are those who trust too much and are therefore too vulnerable. Trust is just an example. To a lesser and greater extent we all view people through the lens of our past experiences, and we need to do this. For instance, it is not appropriate to ask the bus driver to show us his driving licence; we have to take it on trust that he knows what he is doing. The key, though, is to be aware of the patterns we fall into when summing people up, and to learn to hold our views lightly and be more open to finding out about the people in front of us.

A group of people I find I always learn from are children, as they can offer us fresh eyes on the world and a new perspective. A schoolboy chatting to me recently said that he thought sanity is not about how knowledgeable you are, or how 'realistic'. He knows some clever people with first-class degrees and doctorates who have loads of facts at their fingertips; nevertheless, he experiences some of them as less than sane because they cannot relate to others. He also knows some people who believe in things he personally finds odd (like God or homeopathy) and, although he finds their beliefs unrealistic, he finds some of them appear saner than some members of the former group. He thought this was because sanity has more to do with openness and emotional honesty than with leak-proof logic.

The Daily Temperature Reading

Here is an exercise that may help you get more emotional honesty into your relationships. Created by the family therapist Virginia Satir, it is designed to improve your existing relationships; you'll need to persuade your family, friends or work colleagues to do this exercise with you. It is called the Daily Temperature Reading because it takes the temperature of a particular relationship in the here and now. There is a belief that true love, great friendships and good working relationships just happen naturally. Often they do, but this exercise can help the process. It offers ways of confiding in other people, and confiding is an essential element in all kinds of relationships.

First, set aside half an hour when you will not get interrupted. Turn off your phones, computers, televisions. If there are two of you, sit facing each other. If you are a group, sit where you can all see each other. Take a minute or two to contemplate how you feel about yourself and your partner or the group. Like an agenda for a meeting, you have a list of five topics to get through. Try not to stray onto different subjects. The topics are: *i*) Appreciations; *ii*) New Information; *iii*) Questions; *iv*) Complaints with Recommendations for Change; and *v*) Wishes, Hopes and Dreams.

Appreciations

Take turns to share what you appreciate about each other. Be specific and precise. So instead of saying, for instance, 'I love being with you', be specific about what it is you love. For example, 'I love the way you ring me at midday to see how I am. It makes me feel cared for.' When you receive an appreciation, do not argue with it, or bat it back, or immediately say something like, 'Oh, and you too', because this will take away from its impact. Never put a 'but' on an appreciation, or try to sneak in a complaint by saying, for example, 'I would appreciate it if you would . . .' Reserve this section for sharing just what you appreciate about each other. You can decide between yourselves how many turns you wish to take to express appreciation.

New Information

This section is about sharing the events of your lives as well as being open about your moods, feelings and thoughts and about what is affecting them. It is important to keep one another up to date about what is happening to you. This section is for sharing objective information, such as, 'I have a dental appointment tomorrow', and subjective information such as, 'When I lost a tooth yesterday I felt so melancholy, it felt like the beginning of old age. Then I became more hopeful when I realized I still have time left.' The point is to say what is in the foreground for you, and keep it real, even if you have not worked out exactly what it is you are feeling and thinking. It is about not only keeping others informed of new facts but keeping them up-to-date on how you are working things out and what meanings you are making or trying to make. If there is time and if it seems appropriate, you can tell one another how you experienced hearing the information they have shared, or you can simply acknowledge it with a 'thank you' or a nod. If you have observations about what they have said, do not define the other person by making 'you'-statements. You could say, 'I have noticed you say you are sad when . . .' but not, 'You are always sad when . . .' Confine your statements to 'I'-statements, not 'you'-statements.

Questions

What assumptions are you making about your partner or the other people in the group? This is the moment to examine those assumptions. For example, you might say, 'The door slammed when you left the room yesterday. Were you angry or did the wind catch the door and slam it?' When I work with couples I often find that problems arise because they do not examine their own assumptions. Examining our assumptions and checking them out with our partner ensures that we have a relationship with the person instead of a fantasy of them, or avoid falling into the sort of 'I–I' relationship I spoke of earlier. This section is an opportunity to examine your assumptions and ask any type of question. These might be something as mundane as, 'What time are we leaving tomorrow?' or as pertinent as, 'I have experienced you as down and distant this week. Is anything going on?' Asking questions does not mean you will get answers, although you might. It is important to be patient with each other and to foster goodwill. Your question provides information for the other or others as well as being a question in its own right. There is no obligation to answer a question. If you wish, you can merely thank the other for their question, without answering it.

Complaints with Recommendations for Change

Complaints or worries should only be aired in conjunction with a suggestion for how that complaint or worry might be addressed. Without attacking, blaming, name-calling, playing the victim, interpreting or criticizing, describe the behaviour that causes you concern and then explain how it makes you *feel* (not think). Then say what you would like done differently. When you receive a complaint try simply to listen. Do not defend yourself. You do not have to alter your behaviour, although you may choose to. It is not differences that cause problems in relationships but how we deal with those differences. Because of our background and conditioning our response to hearing a complaint about ourselves can be defensive. When a response to someone's concern or complaint exacerbates the situation, the likelihood of a fully functioning relationship is decreased. It may help to remember when you receive a complaint that it is only nominally about you; it is really information about the person making the complaint. When we are able to work through qualms and complaints we can become closer through our successful navigation of the challenge they represent. When someone we love shares a concern, it is vital to develop the habit of listening with empathy and with a desire to understand. An example could be, 'When you come in from work and immediately start relating your day, my train of thought is interrupted, I forget what I was doing and I feel overwhelmed. What I would like would be for you to check in with what I'm doing and let me wrap that up, or mark my place and where I have got up to, and then I really want to hear about your day.' The other might respond with something like, 'I never realized, thank you for letting me know. Just put your hand up to say stop if I'm overwhelming you again.' Other complaints might be more tricky to hear, such as, 'I'm sick of being the person who puts the rubbish out in this house; I want you to do it for a change.' This complaint is expressed with a martyr-ish edge. It might have been better to phrase it as follows: 'As I put the bins out last night, it felt to me as though I am the only person who remembers to do this. Please could you do it next time?' The person on the receiving end may have been about to deliver the very same complaint because they feel that *they* are always left with this chore. Remember: the complaint is about the person making it. The best way to respond is, 'I hear that you feel that it is you who always takes the rubbish out, and you would like to change. Thank you for telling me.' It is best not to argue when you do this exercise. When you next do a Daily Temperature Reading, in the questions section you might say, 'It seems to me we both feel we are doing more than our fair share of chores. Perhaps we need to work out a system or get a cleaner. What do you think?' Remember, the idea is not to fight, and a good relationship is not about determining who is right and who is wrong. It's about finding a way forward together. A common intervention that psychotherapists make when working with couples is to say, 'You can choose between being right, or being together'. As I've said before, bear this in mind if you feel wrongly accused: the accusation is about how the other person feels and they will not feel better if they are made to feel wrong as well.

Wishes, Hopes and Dreams

Some people hold on to a belief that telling others of the things they really want will jinx the dream. In my experience the opposite is more often true. I advocate the sharing of wishes, hopes and dreams in order to get the support and encouragement we need to fulfil them. Before a race an athlete visualizes how he will jump every hurdle and cross the line at the end of the race. He may not win as a result of his visualizing exercise, but he gives himself a better chance of doing so – and so will you, as you share your hopes with others. Sharing our deepest hopes can make us feel vulnerable, so support your partner(s) in this endeavour, rather than challenging them. Sharing our vulnerabilities increases intimacy and deepens the connections between us.

The Daily Temperature Reading can be important to couples, families, work teams and others. To give it a chance, do it, say, every two days for a month as a couple, or weekly for two months as a group. Then evaluate what difference it has made in your lives.

Think about these five modes of communication – appreciating; informing; questioning; complaining and recommending; and sharing your wishes, hopes and dreams – and how you use them outside of the Daily Temperature Reading, in your everyday exchanges. Do you use one mode more often than others? If so, consider using a mode that is not as familiar to you, in order to broaden your range of communication. Think of these five categories, as well, in juxtaposition with Martin Buber's descriptions of types of communication: 'genuine dialogue', 'technical dialogue' and 'monologue disguised as dialogue'. We can make it a goal to make more of our communicating count.

Relating Difficulties: Case Studies

Loneliness and disappointment in relationships can be mitigated if we become mindful of the ways in which we act, and take steps to feel and behave differently. The following two case studies demonstrate how we might go about this.

Zara

Zara was chaotic in her relationships. She was unable to feel secure with a partner and habitually sabotaged her romantic relationships at an early stage, by acting on her feelings instead of first observing them to give herself the chance to choose how she acted. She was twenty-eight and wanted to find someone to spend the rest of her life with. Using self-observation she noticed a certain pattern in her relationships and she noted down the pattern in her diary:

1. She would choose someone who was good-looking and/or charismatic.
2. She would go to bed with him at the earliest opportunity.
3. After sex, she would feel that she was 'in love' with him.
4. She would behave in a 'needy' way and ring him up too much.
5. The relationship died, usually after a couple of months.
6. She would be heartbroken.

This was the hole, the habit, the pattern – whatever you want to call it – that Zara was in.

She made a decision and set out a couple of guidelines for herself. When the next man came along, she would: *a*) not go to bed with him before they had established a relationship; and *b*) not act in a 'needy' way, *even when she felt needy*.

After a while Zara met a man at evening classes who seemed interested in becoming her friend. She did not assume they would become romantic, but they liked spending time together and met up for a drink once or twice a week. This went on for six months. Then they went on holiday together as friends, but came back as lovers. Zara felt the neediness rise up in her. She wanted to know what he was doing and where he was every second of the day: was he thinking about her? But instead of acting on this urge, she exorcised it, to some extent, merely by writing it all down in a private diary. This resolve not to 'smother' the man concerned appears to have been a good guideline, because their relationship continued to deepen, they married and now, decades later, they are still happily together.

So, although I am wary of rules, I have to admit that, in Zara's example, they did allow her to steer her life onto a happier course. Using self-observation you may discover chaotic patterns in your relationship and decide to implement a rule like Zara did, using it as a temporary splint until a more permanent, flexible middle way is found.

Sam

Rather than rules, Sam needed more flexibility in his life. He had rules such as never to talk about the weather, or to even ask the generic question 'How are you?' Sam deemed such ordinary, 'grooming' questions meaningless, and wrote off anyone who used them. His rules made him difficult to get on with and resulted in him living a lonely existence, with little contact with the outside world. He gained some comfort in thinking himself superior to the rest of the population, but feeling superior is no substitute for companionship and the positive difference friends make to a life. Sam became lonely and depressed. When the depression became unbearable he went to see his doctor, who referred him to a counsellor, Simon.

After he had learnt to trust Simon, which took a year of weekly sessions (neural pathways take time to alter), Sam was able to become aware of how he had established his own particular rule book, and how many of his rules were out of date. Supported by Simon, Sam experimented with change and allowed himself more contact with other people. He has not embarked upon a romantic relationship,

nor become a party animal, but he has let a few other people into his life, is less lonely, less rigid and is no longer as depressed.

Philosophers ask themselves the question, 'If a tree falls in the forest but nobody hears it, has it, in fact, made a sound?' I wonder if this question is really asking, 'Would we exist if no one witnessed our existence?' Perhaps we have to ask that, because without another soul or souls to check in with, pass the time with, be affected by and affect, a part of us does seem to diminish. We do feel less human and we are more likely to go insane without the checks and challenges of other good-willed people around us. Solitary confinement is one of the most brutal, most stressful punishments we inflict on our fellow humans. If we are to stay sane, we must not inflict it upon ourselves.

3. Stress

Learning

By improving our self-awareness and prioritizing beneficial relationships, we give ourselves a good chance of holding on to our sanity. Our brains never stop developing and we do have some choices about how they develop. The third cornerstone of sanity is concerned with how we keep our brains – and therefore ourselves – fit.

High levels of stress result in panic or in the brain dissociating. Dissociation is a disconnection amongst our thoughts, sensations, feelings and actions – experienced as a type of blanking out. Therefore high levels of stress are to be avoided. However, no stress at all means that the brain does not get any exercise. A brain is not unlike a muscle, in that the cliché 'use it or lose it' applies. Moderate levels of stress keep our minds in condition, and help us to stay sane. This 'good stress' promotes the neural growth hormones that support learning. Good stress, unlike the type that causes dissociation, can be experienced as pleasurable; it can motivate us or make us curious. More importantly, it triggers neural plasticity, which is why I get excited about it.

In psychotherapy, quite often, what the client and I are working towards is a position where the client is able to tolerate their feelings. We call this 'affect regulation', a process of inhibiting anxiety and fear to allow processing to continue in the face of strong emotion. To work at this level we cannot be too comfortable, because then new learning does not take place; but nor can we be too uncomfortable, for then we would be in the zone where dissociation or panic takes over. Good work takes place on the boundary of comfort. Some psychotherapists refer to this place as 'the growing edge' or 'a good-stress zone', or talk of 'expanding the comfort zone'. The good-stress zone is where our brains are able to adapt, reconfigure and grow. Think of the brain as a muscle and think of opportunities to flex it. The more we flex it, the better our brain functions.

The richer and more stimulating our environment, the more encouraged we feel to learn new skills and expand our knowledge. Such learning seems to have the side-benefit of boosting our immune system. There are some animal studies that show that an intellectually stimulating environment can compensate for the damaging effects of lead-poisoning. Two groups of rats were given water contaminated with lead. One group was put in a stimulating environment and the other was not. Professor Jay Schneider, who conducted the experiment, said that the magnitude of the protective effect of an educationally stimulating environment on the rats' ability to withstand the poison surprised him. I am sad to report the rats in the less stimulating environment did not fare so well. I am the same. When I go away on holiday to a new place I feel refreshed by having been stimulated by new sights, smells, environments and culture. This is an example of good stress. I like to imagine I can feel it doing me good, and the rat experiment suggests that it really might be.

Physical Activity

To stay sane we need to increase the good stress that is generated by engaging not only in more intellectual pursuits but also in physical activity. The brain needs oxygen and the more oxygen it gets the better it functions. Two studies have demonstrated this clearly. In the first, two groups of sedentary elderly people were tested in four areas: memory, executive functioning, concentration, and the speed with which they could perform various physical tasks, from threading a needle to walking along a line. For the next four months, those in the first group walked for twenty minutes a day; those in the second group carried on as normal. Then they were tested again. Group 1 showed significant improvements in the higher mental processes of memory and executive functions that involve learning, planning, organization and multi-tasking. The implication is that exercise might be able to offset some of the mental declines that we often associate with the ageing process. The second study was carried out on patients diagnosed with a major depressive disorder. The first group was given medication alone, the second exercise alone and the third medication and exercise together. The results showed that exercise is as helpful as medication in combating depression, as all three groups showed statistically significant and identical improvement in standard measurements of depression.

It is often the case when we are considering embarking on a new activity (be it ballroom dancing, meditation or other new ventures) that we feel in two minds about it. However, if we *decide* to override that part of us that is reluctant to change (instead of merely *trying to* override it), and undertake a new regime anyway, we give ourselves the chance to experience the difference that new regime makes to us. If we are not feeling more stimulated, more interconnected, more alive, no harm will have been done and we can drop it. Starting a new habit means feeling the impulse to maintain your current way of being, but beginning the new regime anyway: it can feel like a wrench. We usually start to send ourselves messages – like 'this isn't really me' – clock such excuses and decide to persevere with establishing a new habit anyway.

The Nun Study

In his book *Aging With Grace*, David Snowden describes his long-term study of nuns. He undertook the study in order to examine longevity and incidences of dementia. He was also interested in links between the nuns' brain health and factors like intelligence and diet. His subjects provided an ideal opportunity to study the effect of education on long functioning life because the living circumstances of the nuns, in terms of exercise, diet, routine and financial circumstances, were similar, thus making education a measurable distinction between them.

In this study, Dr Snowden noticed that, while some nuns had mentally deteriorated so far that they could no longer live independently or feed themselves, others at the same age or older were still holding down full-time jobs. He found that the nuns who had university degrees had significantly longer, independent, functioning lives than those who had ended their education earlier. And the longer they continued to study, or embark upon and maintain new interests, the more lively their minds seemed to stay.

With another researcher, Jim Mortimer, Snowden also studied 'brain reserve'. They suggested that a brain that has been actively used in socializing and learning all through life builds more neural connections than a brain that has been less stimulated. So, in the former case, when part of the brain is damaged by Alzheimer's, the pathway is not necessarily permanently interrupted, but can find a new route around the tangle or plaque caused by the disease. Snowden and Mortimer also found that some nuns who displayed no signs of Alzheimer's when alive were found to have significant damage caused by it at autopsy, whereas the brains of those who clearly exhibited the condition in life had fewer signs of it when autopsied. Snowden and Mortimer have not yet come to any firm conclusions about the part continuing curiosity and learning plays in building up brain reserve, but circumstantial evidence suggests a connection.

Good stress keeps our brains plastic. A plastic brain can adapt, stay flexible, remain connected to community, and cope with the inevitable changes that life brings. Good stress motivates us by activating our curiosity, firing our enthusiasm and feeding our creativity.

The hormone dopamine is a key neurotransmitter in reward-reinforcement. We can stimulate its production in both healthy and unhealthy ways. The form of dopamine stimulation that I advocate is learning something new, and the thrill that comes with it – whether mastering a new musical instrument, succeeding with a new recipe, shooting a ball into a basket or learning to tell a successful joke. Dopamine production is also stimulated by addictive substances or activities, such as gambling. This is an abuse of dopamine and by using it this way we can overload our systems, causing health and emotional problems. Pleasure is good for us but feeding an addiction is not.

If we are, for instance, hard-working university researchers, we might consider that we are already doing enough learning. It is true that our neural pathways for research will be well developed; but learning how to dance the tango, cook a tagine or speak a new language will supply us with the good stress that builds more brain reserve. However, we need certain conditions for brain building. We must be doing something genuinely new, and we must pay close attention, be emotionally engaged and keep at it. New pathways will form if two or more of these conditions are met, but we will ideally meet all four at once.

Less challenging but also useful are the solo activities sometimes referred to as 'brain training' – such as crosswords, word search games and card games such as solitaire and patience – games that appear to be of limited value as transferable skills. For example, when we learn and practise Sudoku, we get better at Sudoku, but it has limited value that we can integrate into the rest of our life. In fact, as a Sudoku-and-other-numbers-games addict, let me offer a word of warning about such 'brain' games. I have noticed, as I play Bridge or Scrabble against a computer, or Suduko for an hour at a time, that my emotional side feels cut off. As a way of self-numbing I would say that number and letter games could compete with class-A drugs when it comes to shutting down our feelings. It feels to me as though the dopamine kick I get from it has a more addictive edge to it, than a learning edge.

If you too are a games addict, notice the difference in how you feel when instead you read a book. It may feel like it takes more effort, especially when you first start to develop this new habit. A novel, or a book on philosophy, is going to use both sides of the brain: not only will you have feelings about what you read, but your mind will also get more of a work-out because you will make connections between what you are learning and what you already recognize.

When I talk about the benefits of learning, sometimes people confide in me that what stops them embarking on learning something is a sense of shame that they do not know it already. Susan Jeffers wisely said 'Feel the Fear and Do it Anyway'. I say 'Feel the shame and learn something anyway'. No one likes to feel vulnerable[16] but unless we learn to tolerate some emotional vulnerability we will be endangering our growth, and if we do not grow we shrink – and if we do that we jeopardize our sanity.

Recently I was talking to a biologist about the benefits of maintaining the habit of learning. He asked me whether I was right- or left-handed. I said right. He told me that my chances of a full recovery after a stroke would be better if I was left-handed because left-handed people already have more neural connections than right-handed people. He added that if I started the habit of cleaning my teeth or working my computer mouse with my left hand I would begin to build 'brain reserve'. If I later suffered a stroke it would put me in a better position to recover from it.

Whatever new activity we begin to do – from left-handed teeth-brushing, to learning a new language – we will make new neural connections, which can generate greater creativity and new ideas. A new idea has been likened to a shy woodland creature. To coax the shy woodland creature from the shadows into the clearing you must not scare it. Leave a little food for it and it will come out into the clearing where you can see it better. If you treat it well it will not go bounding back into the forest.[17]

Ideas rarely come from doing nothing. We stimulate our brains to come up with ideas when we learn new things or when we rehearse the things we are learning. I ran a five-day group for art students and art lecturers about the psychological processes of creativity. There was a general consensus that ideas came not from sitting around and waiting for inspiration to descend, but from working: trying things out, reading, learning and doing.

Learning Styles

There are many different ways of learning. Some of us absorb best when we read, while others prefer to learn visually from diagrams, videos and demonstrations. Auditory learners prefer to learn through listening, via lectures, talking things through and hearing what others have to say, gaining extra information from the tone and the nuances. There are also kinaesthetic learners, who learn through moving, doing and touching, preferring a hands-on approach through which they actively explore the physical world. So if we have always thought of ourselves as not being able to learn easily, it may be that we have not yet found the style of learning that best suits us; and, as the brain is plastic, we can, with practice, develop new styles of learning. The more we learn, the more we are able, by linking our areas of know-ledge together, to come up with creative ideas. We would not know how physics and sky-diving go together unless we knew a little bit about both. Thus the more we know, the more we can create.[18]

I left school at fifteen and it took me a few years to come around to and enjoy learning. In my early twenties I had a repetitive administrative job. I knew that I felt under-stimulated. Boredom drove me to a College of Further Education recruitment evening. I signed up for Psychology and English A-levels and made new friends at these classes. I remember going round to a friend's house for the first time and being excited by her enthusiasm. She said, 'I'm not bored any more; I find myself thinking about the different motivations of characters in *Twelfth Night*.'

This is what learning does. It gives us more things to think about so we have less time to get bored, depressed and under-stimulated. It builds on our existing knowledge and expands it. It leads us to make more connections by linking together more neural pathways. It also connects our brains to other people's brains.

The next year I did Art and History. These became subjects that I have continued to build on with further reading and, in the case of Art and Psychology, further courses and a degree. Nothing but good has come from my taking a class. One year I did two evening classes, one in Film Appreciation and the other in Creative Writing. In the former I learnt that I disliked listening to people talking about film plots, while in the latter I did much better. In that class I met my husband. Learning new subjects not only builds new connections in our brains, but in our lives as well.

The Comfort-Zone Exercise

Get a large piece of plain paper and draw a circle in the middle. Inside the circle write examples of activities that you feel completely comfortable doing. Around the edge of the circle write down examples of

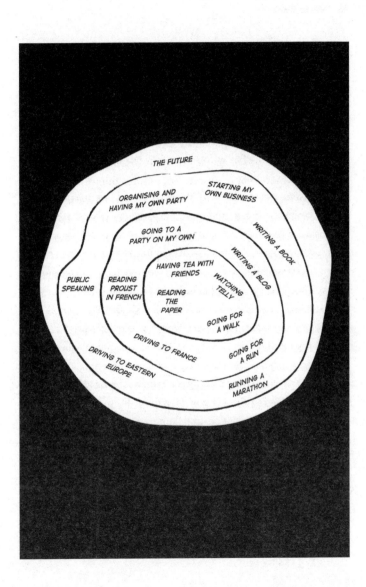

activities that you can do but that you have to push yourself a little bit to do – those activities that may make you nervous in some way, but not so much as to stop you doing them. Draw a larger circle around this circle of activities. In the next band write activities that you would like to do but find it difficult to get up the courage *to* do. Draw another circle around this ring of activities. After that write down those things you are far too scared to try but would like to do. You can create as many circles as you like.

It is useful to consider what we are comfortable with and what we are not, and then to experiment with expanding our area of comfort. We should remember that whatever we try is for ourselves alone. It does not matter what anyone else might think. The idea is to expand our comfort-zone in small steps. We go beyond 'good stress' into 'bad stress' if we attempt too big a leap across zones. When I started to push out my inner circle to gradually include the other zones I felt more confident about all the challenges within that original inner zone. I also found that when I set myself a do-able challenge and succeeded my self-esteem and self-confidence rose in all areas. The greatest leap I made was when I went from not being able to run 100 yards to completing the London Marathon. I am sure this is what gave me the confidence to go on submitting my book, *Couch Fiction,* after its first round of rejections. It was eventually published in May 2010. I have also experienced that if I do not keep on testing my limits, my comfort-zone shrinks back. Challenges that had seemed comfortable one year took courage to achieve the next. I do not want to get into that position again; so, onwards and outwards.

4. What's the Story?

I have included this section on stories because a part of every successful therapy is about re-writing the narratives that define us, making new meanings and imagining different endings. In the same way, part of staying sane is knowing what our story is and rewriting it when we need to.

Our usual emotional, cognitive and physical response to the world – that is, our typical pattern for dealing with recurrent situations – will come from our own stories. Our way of being in the world will also come from stories that we read and that are told to us, from films, sitcoms and the news; they might be family legends, or parables and metaphors, or religious tracts and fairy stories. We make up stories, we read stories, we hear stories. Our lives interweave these stories and respond to them.

Our minds are formed by narratives. We evolved using stories and narratives that are co-constructed. As our earliest caregivers transcribed our sensations, feelings and actions into words for us, our narratives took shape. We used these narratives to integrate our experience into coherent meanings. Children and their parental figures narrate their experience together and, in doing so, they organize their memories and put them into a social context. This assists in linking feelings, actions and others to the self. These co-constructed narratives[19] are central to all human groups – from a family in the western world to the hunter-gatherers of the Kalahari Desert. The co-construction of story has negative and positive outcomes. The downside is that the parental figure can unduly influence the child with his or her own fears and anxieties, prejudices and restrictive patterns of being; but the upside is that co-forming narrative teaches ways of memorizing, as well as imparting positive values, group culture and individual identity. A child not only co-constructs the narrative of his or her life with his or her caregiver, but ideally listens to many other stories as well. We may think this is mainly just for entertainment and bonding, but the repeated telling of stories also helps to form structures in the child's mind that enable problem solving, meaning making, optimism and self-soothing. Wicked witches get their comeuppance, conflicts are resolved and we learn the concept of 'happily ever after'.

In the same way that stories are important in personality formation, they are also significant in the evolution of our species and the creation of culture. Before the invention of writing, stories, sagas and legends were handed down from generation to generation in the form of rituals and oral traditions that contained both education and the foundations of wisdom. Just as new learning forges new neural pathways to what we already know, so a new story adds to our existing stock. The appearance of certain themes across cultures and times – death and resurrection, for instance – testifies to their importance to the species as a whole. Such stories are used to pass down group identity, wisdom and experience for the next generation to build on, as well as giving them ways of coping, self-soothing and facing death.

Stories may unconsciously influence us to act in one way or another, but they also enable us to think about ourselves in an objective way.

When a client in therapy presents a problem, the therapist often asks them to imagine that problem belonging to a friend and, if that was the case, how they would counsel that friend. This use of storytelling helps us to gain some distance from ourselves and gives us perspective. We can also use stories to help us escape into our imaginations when there is no escape in reality. Children often create imaginary worlds where they can succeed and triumph. Though they may be limited in their choices in real life, they can use imagination and storytelling to soothe themselves during real-life experiences that might otherwise be intolerable. It is not only children who can do this. In his book *Man's Search for Meaning*, Victor Frankl explained that while he lived through suffering, atrocity and imprisonment at Auschwitz and other concentration camps he created a place of freedom in his mind and imagination. He ascribes his survival to this act of defiance and hope.

The great thing about a story is that it is flexible. We can change a story from one that does not help us to one that does. If the script we have lived by in the past does not work for us anymore we do not need to accept it as our script of the future. For example, the belief that we are unworthy of being loved and belonging is just that, a belief. This belief, this story we tell ourselves, can be edited. The effects of such editing can be more positively life changing than winning the lottery. Research has shown that after winning the lottery people take about three months to return to the mindset they had before the win. So, if they were generally optimistic and joyful, that's where they return to; and if they were self-loathing and misanthropic, they will be after their win as well. A lot of money does not change our emotional life. The way we talk to and about ourselves and the way in which we edit our own stories, can and does.

Creating a consistent self-narrative that makes sense and feels true to ourselves is a challenge at any stage in life. Our stories give shape to our inchoate, disparate, fleeting impressions of everyday life. They bring together the past and the future into the present to provide us with structures for working toward our goals. They give us a sense of identity and, most importantly, serve to integrate the feelings of our right brain with the language of our left.

Sophie was a fifty-year-old woman who came to see me. She interpreted her life story to mean that she was washed up and on the scrap heap, because 'it's a young person's world'. This worried me because people who interpret events in pessimistic ways are more likely to become depressed and ill, and live shorter lives than those who find positive meanings. Together we worked with her statement, not by arguing about whether it was true or untrue, but by examining how it made her feel and whether further meaning or meanings would not be more helpful. Sophie had just finished a fine-art degree and was finding it tough-going locating places to show her work. I told her a story (more of a myth – I do not even know if it's true) about a telephone-systems salesperson who made a very different kind of sense of rejection. Every time this salesperson was rejected by a prospective customer he was delighted, because it brought him one encounter nearer to his next sale. He calculated his hit-rate as one in fifty cold calls, so if he counted forty rejections he began to get excited, as he knew the sale would be coming soon. This made him more confident. He did very well and won the firm's salesman-of-the-year award. Sophie laughed at the story but it stayed with her and gave her the confidence to tell people that she really wanted to be selected for an artist's residency. When a residency did come her way, she told me, 'I did not have to approach anywhere near fifty people. It was more like seventeen. Holding the story in mind kept me enthusiastic when I talked about my work and what I had to offer.' By telling her story in a different way Sophie changed it, and that in turn changed the way she appeared to others.

We are primed to use stories. Part of our survival as a species depended upon listening to the stories of our tribal elders as they shared parables and passed down their experience and the wisdom of those who went before. As we get older it is our short-term memory that fades rather than our long-term memory. Perhaps we have evolved like this so that we are able to tell the younger generation about the stories and experiences that have formed us which may be important to subsequent generations if they are to thrive.

I worry, though, about what might happen to our minds if most of the stories we hear are about greed, war and atrocity. For this reason I recommend not watching too much television. Research exists that shows that people who watch television for more than four hours a day believe that they are far more likely to be involved in a violent incident in the forthcoming week than do those who watch television for less than two hours per day.[20] Not only does Hollywood supply a succession of movies in which the 'goodies' win by resorting to violence rather than dialogue, but even the news appears to be filtered for maximum emotional shock value, which means it has a bias towards bad news rather than good. Be careful which stories you expose yourself to. I am not saying it is not important to be informed about what is going on, but to be informed repeatedly about bad news will give us neither a balanced view of our world nor of the other people who inhabit it. In contrast to this torrent of bad news, I think it is important to seek out optimistic stories and foster the optimism within ourselves.

I am going to try to convince you that optimism is a good idea.

- Studies show that pessimism in early adulthood appears to be a risk factor for poor physical and mental health later on.[21]
- Optimism is shown to correlate with physical and mental good health.
- Optimistic people recover more quickly after operations and have higher survival rates after cancer. (They are more likely to follow their doctor's orders and so aid recovery.)
- Optimism puts you in a better mood and thereby decreases stress.
- Optimism is correlated with longevity while pessimism is associated with a reduced life span.[22]
- Optimists are more likely to trust others and therefore enjoy more satisfying relationships.
- Pessimists think they are cleverer than optimists but they really aren't.[23]

If I walk into a party with my head held high, with the optimistic attitude that everyone is pleased to see me or would like to meet me (and I them), I will catch someone's eye even if, hitherto, everyone in the room was a stranger to me. I will ask them about themselves and they may ask me about myself; we will probably find some common ground and I might learn something from them as a bonus. But more than that, I give myself the chance of forming what feels like a connection. It might last just a few minutes, or it may be the beginning of a long friendship, but in that connection I feel deeply nourished.

If, on the other hand, I walk into a party with my eyes on the ground, neither interested in meeting anyone nor thinking that anyone would be interested in meeting me, I will not catch anyone's eye and I will not enjoy the party. I will be thinking about ways to leave it. I will not be fully present at the party. Instead I will be present only with my prejudices; I will be projecting a fantasy, or an experience of the past, onto the present, and relating to that, instead of to what is going on around me.

The party is life. Sometimes, I confess, I enter the party in a state nearer the second scenario than the first and sometimes in spite of this somebody is still generous enough to make an effort with me and bring me round. Part of the story I tell myself is that if I am down, other people make me feel better.

What I have displayed here, even in my confessional paragraph above, is optimism. Whether optimism becomes established as a result of good things happening or, conversely, good things happen because they are visualized, hoped for, worked for and obtained, I do not know. But the meanings you find, and the stories you hear, will have an impact on how optimistic you are: it's how we evolved.

What happens if we never hear positive stories? How would it have affected your brain if you had never heard a 'happy ever after' story. If you do not know how to draw positive meaning from what happens in life, the neural pathways you need to appreciate good news will never fire up. Here is a story. A social worker who works with children was working with a family of three siblings aged six, eight and twelve. They had known only their own unsafe home, care homes and foster families all their lives. Their most recent placement was working out extraordinarily well. They had been placed in foster care with a couple, Brianna and Simon, who were empathetic towards the children and gave them some stability. They listened to what the children said, and were good at interpreting the children's feelings and able to provide them with support and loving care. My friend spent some time with them all and wrote her report recommending that the arrangement continue. The children were anxious about the meaning of her visit, so, contrary to usual procedures, she told them what she had written in her report. She said, 'You will not be split up. You are going to stay with Brianna and Simon. We are going to find local schools for you all and, as Brianna and Simon want to adopt you, we are going to begin that process.' The children were silent and seemed stunned, so my friend asked, 'What did I just say?' Each child said, 'We will be split up; we can't stay with Brianna and Simon; there aren't any schools for us and no one will adopt us.' My friend then repeated what she had said, and again the children could not hear it. She tried again and then the youngest child burst into tears. 'Why are you crying, Robbie?' she asked and Robbie replied, 'I think it is because I am so happy.' Eventually they all understood, but found it hard to take in.

The trouble is, if we do not have a mind that is *used* to hearing good news, we do not have the neural pathways to process such news. If we are in this situation we are probably unaware of it, because it is not as though we hear good news and do not trust it. Rather, it is as though we cannot hear good news as good news at all.

How easily do you absorb good news? If good stuff does happen to you, does it make you afraid in any way? Do you perversely comfort yourself by telling yourself it cannot last? If this is the case and if you were to begin to direct your mind to open itself to more optimistic ways of thinking you would probably experience a lot of head chatter telling you to stop. Note the head chatter, expect it and do not let it put you off. We need to point ourselves in the direction of listening for good news. Start a habit of looking for the positives in any situation, however dire. It will feel phoney at first. Often new behaviours feel false because they are unfamiliar; but an optimistic outlook is no more false than always assuming that nothing good will ever happen.

It is not easy simply to turn optimism on. It will take more than deciding that optimism sounds like a good idea. It will take practice and good people around us. You will need to keep up the practice of focused-attention exercises so you can pump up the neural pathways that can steer the mind. You may find that you have been telling yourself that practising optimism is a risk, as though, somehow, a positive attitude will invite disaster and so if you practise optimism it may increase your feelings of vulnerability. The trick is to increase your tolerance for vulnerable feelings, rather than avoid them altogether.

If we practise more optimism, disasters will still happen – but predicting disasters does not make them more tolerable, or ward them off.

At one time, when we went away for weekends, I would be quite low for the last thirty minutes or so of the journey home. I used to imagine that our house had been burgled. I pictured myself ringing the police, getting the broken window boarded up, ringing the insurance company. When I opened the front door, however, I would be delighted and relieved that it had not happened. When I began to practise self-observation, and noticed the fantasies I was having and the stories I was feeding myself, I decided to focus on other things when that particular fantasy visited me, and I was able to minimize the habit. When I got this pessimistic theme under control, I noticed that I not only enjoyed the last thirty minutes of the journey home more, but also the whole weekend. Only when I changed the story did I realize that my fantasy had been a cloud over the whole weekend. Sometimes we only realize that we have been living under a cloud when the cloud is lifted.

Optimism does not mean continual happiness, glazed eyes and a fixed grin. When I talk about the desirability of optimism I do not mean that we should delude ourselves about reality. But practising optimism does mean focusing more on the positive fall-out of an event than on the negative. It does not mean denying that you feel sad that, say, a relationship has not worked out, but rather acknowledging that you are now in a position to have a more successful relationship in the future. I am not advocating the kind of optimism that means you blow all your savings on a horse running at a hundred to one; I am talking about being optimistic enough to sow some seeds in the hope that some of them will germinate and grow into flowers.

The Jack Story

The deserts of America are lonely places; miles can go by without any other cars or a single house. In one of these wildernesses a driver heard his tyre blow. He was more annoyed than worried, knowing that he kept a spare tyre and a jack in his car boot. Then he remembered; he got the jack out last week and forgot to put it back. He had no jack. But things could be worse, because he passed a garage about three miles back. As he started walking, he talked to himself: 'There aren't any other garages around here. I'm at the garage man's mercy. He could really rip me off just for lending me a jack. He could charge me what he wanted. He could charge $50. There is nothing I could do about it. Goddamn, he could even charge $150. People are terrible to take advantage of others like that. Hell, what bastards people are.' He continued absentmindedly telling himself this story until he got to the garage. The attendant came out and said in a friendly way, 'How can I help you?' and the traveller said, 'You can take your damned jack and you can stuff it.'[24]

We can be unaware of the tales we regularly tell ourselves and even unaware of their effect on us. We act on fantasies as though they are realities. And when we visualize something it can happen, because – whether or not we are aware of our fantasies – that is what we expect to happen. We have all heard of people who would really like to have a life partner but tell themselves they cannot trust potential mates. Towards the potential partner they act as though he or she is not to be trusted, and keep testing them: *Would they stay with me if I was really nasty all the time?* They do not mean to do this; they do it because of the story they tell themselves about what others are. Self-fulfilling prophecies are just that: they come true.

Much of the story we tell ourselves goes back to the dynamics of our family of origin. We get fixed in a story like our fellow without a jack and his belief that man always takes advantage of his fellow man. Therefore we need to be self-aware. What stories are we telling ourselves about other people? What dynamic do our stories suck us into, and how do they determine the meanings we put on things and how we define them? We all like to think we keep an open mind and can change our opinions in the light of new evidence, but most of us seem to be geared to making up our minds very quickly. Then we process further evidence not with an open mind but with a filter, only acknowledging the evidence that backs up our original impression. It is too easy for us to fall into the trap of believing that being right is more important than being open to what might be.

If we practise detachment from our thoughts we learn to observe them as though we are taking a bird's eye view of our own thinking. When we do this, we might find that our thinking belongs to an older, and different, story to the one we are now living. For instance, we might be someone like Martin.

Martin always needs an enemy. In every story he tells, there is him and a 'baddie' of some sort. If you hear just one of his stories you might think, 'What a good thing Martin is crusading against such wickedness, be it a corrupt mayor, a political cause, non-paying customer or other scoundrel.' But then you begin to see that every tale features Martin, the crusading hero, against a 'baddie'. The plots of his tales are complex and involve the amassing of evidence on Martin's part. It is amassed through a filter, because once Martin has made up his mind about something, he looks for evidence that backs up his position, and no longer sees anything else. Polarized against the 'baddies' are the 'goodies': if you get into Martin's good books you can do no wrong – his judgement of you will always be positive. When you first get to know him, you may not notice anything amiss, but after a while you may recognize the same patterns reccurring. It seems like the dynamic is already set in Martin's head, and the people around him are simply fulfilling the pre-existing roles he has available. Thus he replays the dynamics of his childhood over and over again. We tend to do the same.

This is why it is important to understand our past. Contemplation, psychotherapy or an exercise like the genogram (which I will describe in more detail later on) can help us do this. Our dynamic is also wrapped up in the stories we tell, the tales we hear and our background fantasies. All this contributes to the meanings we make that shape our behaviour.

A dynamic such as Martin's is usually formed by his childhood experience. Perhaps one or both of his parents had the same dynamic and therefore the same filter through which they viewed the world. Or perhaps Martin's experience was of huge injustice; for example, not being believed when he was telling the truth, or being punished when he was innocent. These grievances fester in the unconscious as: 'I was right; they were wrong.' Indeed 'they' were *so* wrong that Martin needs to keep finding 'them' and *proving* them wrong. He needs to feel himself in the right and be seen to be right, over and over again. So he searches out the enemies and wrongdoers he needs to regulate his own emotions and thus feel okay. He needs an enemy to be 'wrong' so he can feel 'right'. If he sticks to his dynamic unquestioningly he will not develop or learn and the ghosts and stories of his past will prevent him having true contact with people in the present. He will compromise all his relationships.

There are many dynamics that are passed down by previous generations or established by childhood adaptations to an environment that the individual no longer inhabits. An example is our attitude to money: we may be striving for money at the expense of our relationships, or believe we have less or more than we actually do. Money is often a metaphor for how secure we feel in our relationships. For example: if we cannot face up to our fear of losing love, we displace that fear by reiterating reasons to be mean with our money.

Then there are our attitudes to place. If we are always moving, never satisfied with this town or that house, this country or that continent, and come up with brilliant reasons as to why we need to move again, the solution is probably to be found in our own psyche, rather than in the geography of a particular place or the ways of its inhabitants.

There are any number of examples I could come up with to illustrate stuck patterns of thinking, reacting and doing, to show how we use reason to prevent us from discovering more about our feelings. We need to look at the repetitions in the stories we tell ourselves about other people – at the *process* of the stories rather than merely their surface content. Then we can begin to experiment with changing the filter through which we look at the world, start to edit the story and thus regain flexibility where we have been getting stuck.

In my personal therapy I uncovered many such stories and was able to trace the origins of some of them. When exploring my patterns for acting in groups, I used an exercise called the genogram. A genogram is an elaborate family tree, which traces not only blood lines, but lines of behaving, relating, character traits and attitudes. I have explained how to create a genogram in the exercise section at the back of this book. Looking at my genogram I saw that both of my parents come from large families. Then there was something I had not noticed before, which became obvious once it was on paper in front of me: both of my parents had a sibling to whom they were apparently less close than to their other siblings. Both of my parents also idolized one of their own parents.

Then I looked at the way I myself behaved in group situations. In psychotherapy training you usually belong to many groups: your main training group, plus different groups for different modules of the training. I noticed that I always idealized one member of each group and felt annoyed by or dismissive of another. It came as a revelation to me that this pattern was repeated in all my groups, and it dawned on me as I worked with my genogram that I had a pattern for behaving in these group situations that might be embedded in the past rather than be a response to the given situation in the present.

Once I discovered this I had more choice about how to act. Rather than letting that behaviour continue automatically, I resolved to observe the impulses I had to admire one person and demonize another. If I found myself demonizing a person I practised focusing on what was positive about them. By doing this I changed my negative filter for a positive one. Sometimes it is necessary to over-steer in the opposite direction for a while, in order to find your true trajectory.

The next group I engaged with was an interview panel for a new job. I had applied for my first job as a therapist, at a centre for recovering drug and alcohol addicts, where I would have to run therapy groups. The interviewer asked me what my group style was. I told them how I had traditionally behaved in group situations and I expected it to cost me the job. However, I did get it. I told them I was surprised, considering I had revealed my habit of favouritizing and demonizing in groups. The supervisor told me that it was because I was *aware* of this impulse that she had faith that I would not act on it, and that is why they considered me a safe group leader. After that trust was shown towards me,[25] I did not act on my old impulse, even though I still felt its pull. I was able to do that because

I had learnt to stop and observe my instincts, rather than unthinkingly going along with them. In this way I changed the story of how I act in groups.

As I have said previously, sometimes a new behaviour feels false or unreal but is merely unfamiliar. In my experience what 'feels' true might not actually be the truth, or good for us; it might merely be familiar. And, conversely, what feels 'false' might not be; it might just be new. I can sometimes still feel a compelling impulse to demonize and idolize members of a group, and if I give into it, it feels temporarily satisfying. It takes willpower and practice to be aware that I feel the impulse; it feels more comfortable to ignore it. But, gradually, resisting those impulses becomes my nature too. I can free myself from an old dynamic. I can let neural pathways laid down in my childhood relationships grow over, and I can forge new paths over uncharted territory, paths that serve me, the people around me, and possibly the world, more advantageously. Although we are always in danger of reverting to old unsatisfactory patterns, especially in times of stress, new behaviour can become automatic too, and loses its 'phoney' feel.

Each of us comes from a mother and a father, or from a sperm bank, and each of us was brought up by our parents or by people standing in for them. Many of us have siblings, uncles, aunts and cousins. All of these people have an impact on who we are, as do their ancestors. Those ancestors, too, had problems and triumphs, and any learning or habits these experiences gave them they tended to pass down. Red hair or skin tone are easily spotted as inherited characteristics, and it's not difficult to spot, for instance, an inherited aesthetic taste. Using the genogram we can see how we form and

keep (or do not keep) relationships, how we act in groups, how we make decisions and use thought and emotions, and generally find our place in the world. In the genogram these inherited characteristics are as obvious as hair-colour or sense of taste. The point of the exercise is to free you up to make more appropriate choices, so that it is YOU who is making the choices that affect you, and not your great-grandparents. You may feel it is ridiculous to think that your ancestors are influencing you now, but part of who we are derives from previous generations, in ways that can be either productive or unproductive. You can find exact instructions for the genogram exercise at the end of the book.

Through the millennia, stories, songs and rituals have been passed down by the elders to the young of our tribes. Some of the stories and their meanings get lost. I wonder what else is lost with them? In an age of 24/7 news we tend to be all-consumed with the stories of the here and now; the ever unfolding crises and negative things happening in the world. Do our elders still want to tell their stories? Do we still know how to listen if they do? And if we do not, what are we hearing instead?

I am going to finish with a couple of stories that illustrate, first, how change can come about through dialogue and, second, how wisdom is passed from one generation to another.

Die Meistersinger: *The Master Singers*

Die Meistersinger von Nürnburg is an opera by Wagner. It is a story about a singing competition. The Meistersinger ('master singers') is a guild-like institution that runs the competition according to strict, pedantic, unbending rules that provide structure and discipline but stifle creativity and joy. Enter Walther the romantic genius, whose chaos injects brilliance, originality, passion, artistic integrity, erotic feeling and, unfortunately, a riot into the proceedings. Here we have the two elements of life we must steer between: rigidity, represented by the Meistersinger, and chaos, represented by Walther.

The hero of the opera is Hans Sachs, a cobbler, who persuades the Meistersinger that rules are only useful if they are flexible and applied when real need arises. Sachs listens to both sides, appreciates their opposing points of view and engages them in dialogue. He is a learned and thoughtful man who understands the need to steer a course between chaos and rigidity. We see him pondering man's illusions and the madness of human existence and wondering how to apply philosophy to the problem of getting the Meistersinger to appreciate Walther's merits and Walther to see the necessity of some rules to preserve the history and story of their country. Thanks to his thoughtful, reflective and flexible thinking and his wisdom, all ends well. Only one of the Meistersinger, Beckmesser, remains unconvinced and unchanging. Beckmesser is tripped up by his own self-interest. He tries to cheat and ends up isolated and unhappy. Sachs, unlike Beckmesser, understands that there is no shortcut to flexibility; it demands integrity, hard work and close attention. Our job is like Sachs's. We too, have to negotiate that line between rigidity and chaos.

My Wooden Spoon

I sometimes look at a busy street and think: in a hundred years, we will all be dead. On this same street a hundred years ago, perhaps another woman thought the same thing. Perhaps, however, like me, she consoled herself with the thought that love is generative and lives on in the next generation, passed on in the habits of love we inculcate in our pupils, children and friends. I have my late aunt's paintings around me, my late mother's ring on my finger and her words inside me still urging me to tell my daughter to 'be careful' every time she leaves the house. My grandfather's gruff sarcasm lives on in my father and in me, so he is not really dead. When my daughter lays out a sewing pattern, my fondness for needlework lives on in her.

This deeply moving process, that connects human to human in a cascade of memory passing through generations, can be symbolized by particular objects that are passed down along with the knowledge of our ancestors. I am the proud owner of a wooden spoon that is worn into an un-spoon-like stump. In the pre-electric whisk days of the 1960s, my aunt taught me to cream the butter and sugar for a cake mixture; we always used the same spoon. Even then the spoon was worn out. My aunt had, in her turn, used it as a child. I use a whisk now; but the sight of that spoon in the drawer brings tears to my eyes if it catches me unawares on an hormonal day. My aunt will be forgotten eventually; my daughter may not talk about her to her children; but I am sure that my daughter will teach her own children how to make cakes. Along with cake recipes she will pass down the love I received first from my aunt. Oh yes, my aunt will live on, even if her name gets mentioned less and less and her spoon is thrown away.

Conclusion

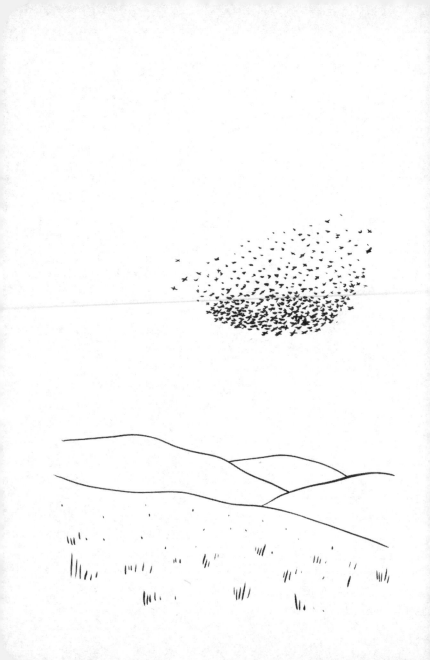

So how do we stay sane? We can develop our faculties of self-observation so that we can have the capacity to observe even our strongest emotions, rather than being defined by them, allowing ourselves to take in the bigger picture. Self-observation helps us to avoid too much self-justification and getting stuck in patterns of behaviour that no longer work for us. We can prioritize nurturing relationships and allow ourselves to be open. We can relate – not as who we *think* we should be, but who we actually *are*, thus giving ourselves the chance to connect and form bonds with others. We can seek out 'good stress' to keep our minds and bodies fit for purpose, and we can be watchful of the stories we hear and the belief systems we live our lives by. We can edit our story at any time, to right ourselves if we veer off course either into chaos or rigidity.

Is it that easy? No, it isn't. One of the things that can give us the illusion of sanity is certainty; yet certainty is a trap. On the other hand, we can swing too far in the opposite direction and become so unsure that we never set off on any path. Extremes appear not to be the best way forward for sanity. I say make a mark, put a foot onto the path, see (and feel and think) how it lands; and then you can make a good guess about where to put the next foot. And if you start to go off in the wrong direction, it is never too late to change course.

I hope reading about how to stay sane has been helpful. To get more out of this book, work through the exercises in the next section.

Exercises

I hope that this book will be useful to you, even if all you do is read it. However, in order to make connections, reading on its own is rarely enough. To really take on board the lessons in this book it is necessary to work experientially. It is one thing to know about something and another to embody it. In order to embody the habits of self-observation it is necessary to practise them; merely knowing about them is not enough. The point of a set of instructions that comes with a model-aeroplane kit is not to supply you with reading material, but to guide you in the practical steps you need to apply in order to build the kit. This exercise chapter is similar to such instructions. The exercises are not simply for reading, they are for doing. Either tackle these exercises on your own, with another person or in a group. Do not tackle too many exercises at once. Personally, one per day would be enough for me: this gives me time to allow insights to come up from the unconscious, and for any self-adjustment to take place.

1. The One-Minute Exercise

For sixty seconds focus all your attention on your breathing. Breathe normally and return your attention to your breath whenever it wanders, without trying to change how you are already breathing. Attempt this without thinking in words.

It takes years of practice before we can maintain this sort of alert, clear attention for even a single minute. This is not an exercise at which you can fail. It is about your experience of the practice. This simple breathing exercise provides a foundation for subsequent exercises, but do not wait until you can achieve it before trying other exercises. Simply return to it often.

When one minute is up, notice how the exercise was for you. How did directing your focus feel? Did you notice a change in mood? How did doing the exercise affect you and how long do its effects last?

2. The Thirty-Minute Exercise[26]

- Commit to doing this exercise and allotting the full thirty minutes to it.
- Get yourself a notebook and something to write with.
- Turn off the phone, computer, radio and television. Resolve not to pick up a book or a newspaper, and choose a time when you will not be disturbed.
- Get yourself a clock or stopwatch and set it for 30 minutes.
- Sit with your back supported. You can put your feet up but do not lie down, as you may go to sleep, which is not the purpose of this exercise.
- Focus your attention on your breathing and empty your mind of other thoughts.
- Thoughts will come into your head but do not stay with any

one thought. Label it and write it on your pad with one or two words, then let it go. When the next thought comes into your mind, do the same thing. If the urge to stop the exercise comes into your mind, treat that like any other thought, jot it down and focus your attention back on your breathing.

- Do this for thirty minutes.

Now look at all the thoughts you have written down, sort them into one of the following categories and then total the thoughts in each category. The numbers at the end of each category are my own results for this exercise:

- Sensory-awareness thoughts: e.g. sounds, sights smells sensations – 4
- Planning thoughts: to-do lists of wants or needs – 3
- Anxiety-provoking thoughts: worries or self-deprecating thoughts – 2
- Playing back of memories – 0
- Fantasies about non-existent situations, relationships or events – 0
- Envious, angry, rebellious, critical thoughts: wanting to stop the exercise or critical thoughts about others – 5
- Take-over: any thoughts you were unable to clear and that took over the exercise? – 0

You can add more categories to suit the types of thoughts you have.

The aim of the exercise is first to see what happens for you; for you to notice how you experience the exercise. You are probably pretty good at noticing the words you use as you talk to yourself, but it is interesting to listen to those thoughts that do not have words.

Secondly, this thirty-minute sample of your thoughts might be an indication of the percentage of your daily thoughts in the various different areas; so, for example, if you spend 80 per cent of your thinking life in fantasy and 20 per cent feeling critical, you can look at that and think: 'I have a choice. I may want to experiment. Perhaps it would be more satisfying to allot more of my thinking time to noticing what I can see or smell or if I focused instead on what I appreciate?' The point of the exercise is to become more self-aware. You cannot change anything unless you know what it is you are changing. The only way you can get this exercise wrong is to not do it, or abandon it early. But even then you can start again.

This is an extract of the summary I made and the conclusions I came to when I had finished the exercise:

I do not know which category to put my fleeting thought about appreciating marmalade in; maybe it should have gone in memory rather than sensory awareness. Anyway, don't suppose that matters. I notice I've written 'too fat' down; can't remember having that thought, but I'm guessing I was thinking about myself – that definitely goes in 'Anxiety-provoking'. I had quite a lot of resistance to doing the exercise – five protests, I notice on the pad. The other thing I noticed is that all the protests happened in the first ten minutes and that the first half seemed to go slowly; then I surrendered to the exercise and the second half almost went too fast, and I was sorry when it was over. After I had finished resisting it, it felt as if I was keeping myself company and that was a good feeling. I wonder if that was because I was then open to what popped into my head? I'm not sure what that resistance is about but it felt very familiar. Next time I feel that resistance I will be curious as to what it is about; whether it is a matter of long-term gain or short-term gain. In this instance I feel satisfied that I listened to it but put it on one side. Had I acted on it, it could be seen to be self-sabotaging. I do find it incredible how a simple exercise like this really does feel like I paid myself some positive attention and gained from it. I'm not sure whether the meanings I have extracted are anything more than post-rationalization, but appreciating that can be satisfying too.

This exercise gives us information about ourselves that we may not otherwise have appreciated. When we do the exercise once a week and compare the results, we can monitor changes in our thinking patterns. It also lets us get a feel for which thoughts foster our creativity and curiosity and may lead to growth, and those that, by contrast, lead us down the dead-end of post-rationalization.

3. A Self-Observation Exercise to Do Whilst Working

Try this: When you are next doing chores around the house – cooking, cleaning, washing, etc. – focus with complete awareness on what you are doing, mentally recording each feeling, thought, sensation or memory as it enters your head. For example, 'Now I am washing a cup; I feel the warm water and soapy suds; now I'm putting the cup on the draining board and noticing the sound of one against the other; now I am thinking about the war in Afghanistan; now I am pulling the plug', and so on. You might want to have a shower with complete awareness, or wash the kitchen floor, or eat a meal. This is a simple way to develop self-observation and concentrate on living in the moment.

4. The Focused-Attention Exercise

For this exercise I like to take between forty-five minutes and an hour, but you may want to start with five minutes of focusing, and build up in increments. It may help to have someone read this exercise to you while you are doing it, or you can record yourself reading it aloud, and play it back.

Think of this as a work-out for your brain, so do not go to sleep. Sit on a chair with your back straight, your feet on the ground and your eyes open. First, and without changing it, notice how you are breathing . . . When your mind wanders, and it will, bring it back to your breathing . . . Notice how your abdomen expands as you breathe in . . .

Looking down at the ground in front of you, notice what your eyes alight upon; become aware of the colours, textures and shapes you can see . . . Spend a minute or two looking and noticing without judging what you see . . . Return your attention to your breathing . . . Imagine the shape the air makes inside your body . . . Notice the in-breath . . . Notice the out-breath . . .

Notice all the sounds you hear . . . Notice the sounds outside the room . . . Notice the sounds in the room . . . Spend a couple of minutes alternating your attention between all the different sources of sound you can hear . . . Now return your attention to your breathing . . . Notice the sensation of your out-breath as the air leaves your nostrils . . . Notice the different sensation of the air coming into your nostrils on your in-breath . . . Be aware of any taste in your mouth and smells in the room . . . on your in-breath, pay attention to smell . . . and on your out-breath pay attention to taste . . . Where on your tongue is the sensation of taste happening? . . . At what point in your cycle of breath is your sense of smell heightened? . . .

Come back to your breathing again . . . Imagine the clean air travelling through your body to your feet . . . Be aware of what the soles of your feet feel like . . . What does the skin on your feet feel right now? . . . Where is most pressure felt on the feet? . . . Then pay attention to what the skin feels on your right hand . . . What, if anything, is it touching? . . . Now turn your attention to your left hand . . . Think about the external temperature your hands can sense . . . Return to your breath . . . If your eyes are not closed close them now, as you notice how you are breathing . . .

Turn your attention to your digestive system . . . Move your awareness slowly through your mouth . . . oesophagus . . . stomach . . . intestines . . . bowel . . . bladder . . . rectum . . . Come back to your breathing, notice your in-breath . . . then your out-breath . . . Notice the turn at the top of the breath . . . How long do you take after breathing in before the out-breath starts? . . . Be aware of that pause . . . Be aware of the pause at the bottom of the breath . . . Now take your awareness to your heart . . . notice your pulse . . . stay there for a while, focusing on your heartbeat . . . Return to noticing your breathing and pause there for a minute . . .

Focus on the chatter in your head; spend a while observing the thoughts you are having . . . Come back to your breathing . . . Now imagine yourself being able to breathe underwater, like a fish . . . Imagine yourself deep in the ocean, looking up to the surface of the water . . . That surface is your mood . . . Is it stormy? . . . Smooth? . . . Now you are a bird flying high above the water . . . With the power of your thought you can make the water rough or smooth . . . Return your attention to your breathing . . .

Now turn your inner focus to the person who is closest to you at the moment . . . How do you relate to that person? . . . How do you feel when you think of them? . . . Broaden the net to those you have spoken to today . . . Do you feel connected or disconnected to them? . . . How do you feel connected or disconnected to your closest family and friends? . . . To your community? . . . Your country? . . . Your world? . . .

Come back to your breathing once more, be aware of the rise and fall of your breath. Remember what you have just done; you have explored your five most immediate senses: sight, sound, touch, taste and smell. You have explored inner, physical sensations and you have noticed your thoughts and your feelings. You have visualized your feelings as the surface of the ocean while you have observed them; you have felt your sense of connectedness with others, and now you return to your breathing once more . . .

As you notice your breathing, notice yourself noticing your breathing . . . Notice that you can focus your attention purposefully to any of these areas . . . You are not at the mercy of your thoughts, you can direct them . . . You can deliberately notice something . . . or you can deliberately or absentmindedly notice your attention wandering . . .

Write or draw what it was like for you to do this exercise. What is in the foreground for you now, as you remember doing it?

5. The 1 2 3 4 Breathing Exercise[27]

Sit supported or lie down. Become aware of your breath. As you breathe, give each stage of your breathing a number:

1, *Inhale*
2, *Top of in-breath*
3, *Exhale*
4, *Bottom of out-breath*

Get used to counting with the breath. If you spend too little time at the top or at the bottom of the breath to apply numbers 2 and 4, slow yourself down until you are counting and breathing easily.

Now, as you count and breathe, bring in the observing part of your mind. Notice the subtle differences of emotion you experience with each stage of the breath. First of all, compare 1 and 3, then compare 2 and 4. Notice which is the most comfortable stage of the breath cycle for you and which is the least comfortable. Spend as much time as you need to do this.

When we have become aware of the nuances of our emotion on each number, we are going to exchange the numbers for a mantra. So you get the whole phrase in, you might need to lengthen the breath; if you are breathing slowly and have plenty of time, do not feel the need to speed up. Replace the numbers with the following phrases:

1, *I take from the world*
2, *I make it my own*
3, *I give back to the world*
4, *I come back to myself*

You can think about whether the phrases correlate with the moments of the breath cycle when you felt most and least comfortable, and whether there is any new information for you there. You can also use these mantras to meditate upon any interaction about which you feel self-righteous or otherwise emotionally charged. For example:

1, *(breathing in) I noticed someone taking my parking space (I take from the world)*
2, *(top of the breath) I imagined they did it on purpose to spite me (I make it my own)*
3, *(breathing out) I shouted at them not to park there (I give back to the world)*
4, *(bottom of breath) I felt self-righteous (I come back to myself)*

Then you could use the mantra to think about what you will do differently afterwards:

1, *(breathing in) I will notice someone taking my parking space (I take from the world)*

2, *(top of the breath) I will not take this personally (I make it my own)*

3, *(breathing out) I tell them I have paid for the space and public parking is around the corner; I make a bigger sign for the space (I give back to the world)*

4, *(bottom of breath) I feel satisfied (I come back to myself)*

A more positive example could be:

1, *(breathing in) I was taught by my aunt to bake (I take from the world)*

2, *(top of the breath) I made up my own recipes (I make it my own)*

3, *(breathing out) I pass my learning on (I give back to the world)*

4, *(bottom of breath) It feels good (I come back to myself)*

When discovering these exercises you may alight on a favourite. The 1234 Breathing Exercise is mine. I do it at least once a week and usually more often. I love how, for me, it mirrors the experience of being alive, of taking in or reaching out and then returning to the self. It also mirrors how we each put our own particular spin ('I make it my own') on what we perceive.

6. The Crowded-Place Exercise (Feeling, Thinking, Acting)

The Crowded Place Exercise helps us discover which 'being zone' is our most comfortable. To use ourselves optimally we need to be operational in three 'being zones': thinking; feeling; and taking action. Normally we are more comfortable in one or two of these zones. The Crowded Place Exercise may help us become aware of which zone we go to first, and remind us to use all three zones in order to maximize our inner resources.

To start with, do this exercise quickly, without rereading each part. You will need something to write with and your notepad (or write the answers on this book). Your answers do not need to be long. You are looking for first impressions here, not deliberations. (I have used the pronoun 'I' throughout the exercise – the 'I' is you and not me!)

i.

- I am imagining I am in a crowded place. I am feeling ....
- In this crowded place, I have my family and friends near me and I feel ....
- The crowd surges forward and somehow I become separated from my group. I feel ....
- I am surrounded by hundreds of people but I am on my own. I feel ....
- The crowd disperses and I am on my own. I feel ....

ii.

- I am in a crowded place. I think ....
- I have my family and friends near me. I think ....
- The crowd surges forward and somehow I become separated from my group. I think ....
- I am surrounded by hundreds of people but I am on my own. I think ....
- The crowd disperses and I am on my own. I think ....

iii.

- I am in a crowded place. What I do next is ....
- I have my family and friends near me. What I do next is ....
- The crowd surges forward and somehow I become separated from my group. What I do next is ....
- I am surrounded by hundreds of people but I am on my own. What I do next is ....
- The crowd disperses and I am on my own. What I do next is ....

Now answer these questions:

- Thinking back over this visualization, did you see yourself as a child, one of the adults, or the person most in charge of the group?
- Do you think it is important that you stick to the role you imagined for yourself?
- How much difference was there between the feeling, thinking or doing answers? (If the answers were the same go back and do it again!)
- Which came easiest to you, the feeling, thinking or doing answers?
- How flexible or rigid are you about what responses you have? Do you see that you have a choice? Or is there no choice in how you respond?
- Do you believe that your thinking influences your feeling and doing. Or does your feeling influence your thinking and doing? Or for you, is it doing that seems to come first followed by either feeling or thinking?
- Which would you say was your most dominant zone of being: feeling, thinking or doing? And your least practised zone of being?
- If you think about some of the other choices that affect how you act, think or feel, and imagine yourself doing them, how does that feel?
- If you think of the days ahead, what choices do you have in how you think, feel and act? Patterns of behaving are habitual, but what is it like just to play in imagination about changing some of those patterns?

- What would the pattern look like with one or two very minor changes?
- What would major changes look like?
- How many of your answers reflected pessimism?
- How many of your answers reflected optimism?

iv.
- Feel your response to doing this exercise.
- Think about your response to doing this exercise.
- *Did* you do this exercise? Do you often miss out the 'doing' in your life? Is it a pattern?

This exercise may help us to become aware of which 'being zone' we go to first and remind us to use all three zones – thinking, feeling and taking action – in order to maximize our inner resources.

I also use this exercise when working with couples or groups, to discover which zone each person is most comfortable in. When this is understood and communicated, people can better understand each other and improve their relationships. For example, I asked one couple I was working with to describe to me a typical argument between them. They told me they were expected at a friend's house for the weekend. Their host had said, 'Start out after breakfast and I'll see you when I see you.' The man assumed this meant everyone in the car by half past eight, ready to hit the road. The woman had assumed it meant she could give the kids some cereal in front of their cartoons while she leisurely packed, listening to her favourite Saturday-morning radio show. By nine o'clock, seeing the rest of the family still in their pyjamas, he started to raise his voice and she responded in kind.

The man was a 'do-er' and the woman was a 'feel-er', but they did not understand this, and found each other's approach to this everyday situation incomprehensible. Doing the Crowded Place Exercise with each other, and learning that they each had a particular 'being zone' that was more developed than the other zones, helped them better understand each other and predict each other's responses to situations. This allowed them to be more specific in what they each needed and to come to a compromise – not because one of them was right and the other wrong, but because they had come to respect that they were different and that each needed to consider the other accordingly.

7. The Genogram Exercise

This exercise can take anything from a couple of hours to a week, depending on how much time you give it. It is best not to rush it, so attempt it when you have the time to do it justice. The genogram is probably one of the most comprehensive tools to aid self-awareness that exists, giving you nearly as much insight into yourself as you might get from a good therapist. But it comes with a warning. Look after yourself while you do it. Listen to your instinct. If you feel overwhelmed by the information you are uncovering, take that feeling seriously and take a break or stop. You can always come back to it later, or when you have more support.

i.

In the centre of a massive piece of paper draw a horizontal line. At each end of it put a very short vertical line – to a small square for your father on one end and, on the other end, to a circle for your mother.

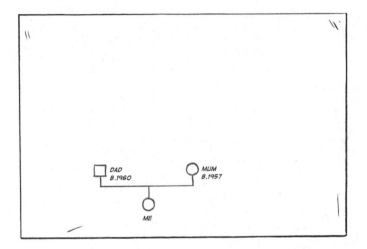

If you were brought up by a gay couple, that would be two circles for two women or two squares for two men. Put their names next to their symbol and their birth date. If either one of them has died put an X through the circle or square and put in their date of death. If there has been a divorce or a separation mark the date of that with a double dash through the horizontal (marriage) line.

ii.

Next, put yourself and your siblings on the map, squares for males, circles for females. Put a star in your own circle or square, because you are starring in this exercise. Put in any miscarriages as a little dot.

iii.

Now put in your grandparents. Put in your aunts and uncles, in the right birth order. I'm not saying this is an easy thing to do, but keep

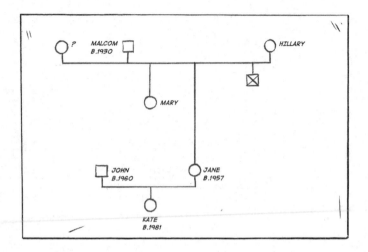

at it. It's at this stage I usually start again, on an even bigger piece of paper. Now you'll have a map of your closest relatives, parents, siblings, grandparents, aunts and uncles.[28] Now add your relatives by marriage and any additional blood relatives – your children, your nephews, cousins, nieces; include them all. Pick five adjectives to describe each person – get other members of your family to help you, but avoid sentimental nostalgia and be realistic.

iv.

If an individual has had more than one marriage or live-in partnership, show this by extending the marriage lines. Put in any non-relatives who lived with your family, such as a lodger or anyone who was especially important to you or your family – maybe with a line of a different colour.

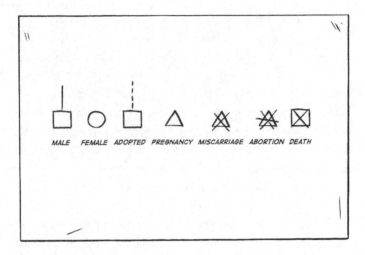

Here are all the symbols you need on the maps. As you can see, you use different lines between two people to show if a relationship was close or conflicted, violent, loving, and so on.

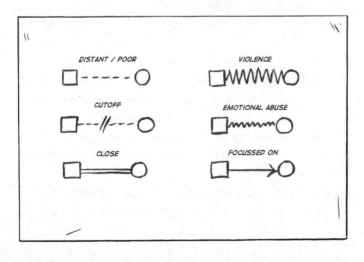

As you create the family genogram, what are you noticing? What are your feelings? Are you fascinated or do you want to push it away? Try not to interpret or give explanations for the feelings straight away, but stay with those feelings. By doing this exercise you will be recovering impressions, memories and associations. Invisible messages, such as who you feel able to confide in and who you do not, will be filtering down to you as you create the genogram. You can keep all of these overt and hidden messages in mind and decide which you need to maintain and which you want to become more aware of, so that you can understand the impact your family or origin are having on your life now.

Think about the important choices you have made about wanting, or not wanting, to be defined by what you experienced and noticed in your family. Make a list of these things. Have these choices changed since you first made them? Which ones still operate in your life? Looking at these past relationships, can you trace how they may be affecting your current relationships?

Here are some further questions which you may wish to consider:

- Which family member or members are you most similar to? Which of their qualities do you closely identify with?
- Think about the earliest messages you got from each family member. What do you think is important in life? Where have your rules for living come from? For example, how much do you feel you can reveal about yourself to other people? Where does your openness, or your reserve, come from?
- How is love expressed in your family? How is caring shown? What happened if someone needed extra help in your family?

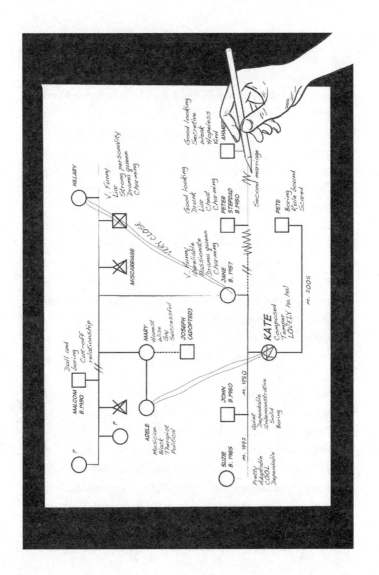

Who did they go to, and how did they get support? When you need support how do you get it?

- How were emotions expressed in your family? How were emotions contained in your family? How were emotions repressed in your family?

- How were the children treated and brought up? How were they disciplined?

- What is your fantasy of a happy family? How does this compare to the reality represented in the genogram?

- What did your parents get right?

- How have the various family members related to each other, and how has that affected your life?

- Look for family crises. Is there a pattern? Have there been any complete breakdowns of contact between siblings, for instance? Bankruptcies? Other disasters? Can you identify patterns of blaming? What are the patterns for chaos in your family?

- What are the patterns for divorce in your parents' family? What are they in your family?

- Look at the patterns of the relationships between all the people on your map. Who got on? Who was estranged? Is there always someone who seems to have to play the role of the scapegoat – the outcast? Is there a culture of favouritism, too?

- Who has had mental-health problems in your family? Looking at the mental-health problems through the generations, does it seem to come from family traits or from outside events? What evidence is there of the effect of traumatic experiences being passed down generations?

- Look at your own relationship between you and your mother. Look at her relationship with her own mother. Do the same for your father and his father. Look at their relationships with both their parents.

- What is the pattern of the relationship to authority in your family? What were your grandparents' individual relationships with authority like? Your parents? Yours? How have their relationships with authority impacted upon yours? Repeat this question with regard to the opposite sex, ethnic minorities, poor people, rich people, foreigners, etc.

- How did the patterns you have noticed help to shape your character, your identity?

- What are the beliefs about the 'right way' of doing things in your family? What is the right way to make small talk or embark on a romantic relationship, for instance? What are the shared values, spoken and unspoken?

- Do you feel in debit or credit, as far as affection and attention go? Do you feel understood by or unknown to your family of origin?

- How were the expectations you have of relationships formed?

- Are there any jobs or occupations that each generation seems to take up? What feelings do you have about the passing on of hobbies or professions?

- How do the people on the genogram talk about the other people on the genogram? Have you noticed that before? How has it influenced how *you* talk about other people?

- What was it like to be with your siblings when your parents were not present? Who played what role? Were you dismissed or valued? Who held the limelight? Who disappeared into the shadows? How has being a member of all these different-size groups affected you today? Do you feel there is safety in numbers? Or do you feel cowed by large groups? Are you fine being with one other person while feeling threatened in a three? If it is hard for you to be in a group today, can you trace where this came from by looking at your family genogram?

- What are the stories that the older generation frequently told the younger generation? Are you passing them on in your turn? Are there similar rhythms to the stories you tell each other? Do you tell no stories at all?

- How did your parents use television? Has this been passed down? Think about how food has been eaten in your family. Sitting around a table as a group? In front of the television? Or are family meals never taken?

- What has been your ancestors' attitude towards religion? How has this affected you?

- How open or how secretive has your family been? With each other? With people beyond the family? What is your own attitude towards secrets?

- What is the emotional legacy you have inherited? Which ways of believing, behaving, thinking and feeling have you inherited from your ancestors?

- What has been your conditioning as to the right and wrong ways of doing things?

- Was thinking more highly regarded than feeling or doing in your family? Or was being able to emote or to act given more approval? What is the legacy of this for you?

- What stands out as the most important (positive and negative) things you have learnt from being in your family?
- What are the male and female attitudes to work in your family? To money? To sex?
- What part does immigration or emigration play in your family? Or staying put? How does this affect you today?
- How are you tackling this exercise? How do you imagine your ancestors' attitude towards it would have been?

These questions are not exhaustive. If other questions and lines of enquiry have come up for you, pursue them. These are just examples of questions you can answer more fully with the help of your genogram. Draw and write on it. You may want to create several with different themes.

From the genogram you may be able to remember stories and family legends that are not toxic, but that nurture and nourish. Every family is a mixed bag and it's important not to throw away the good as we pick out the less helpful myths we have overtly and covertly been told.

I compare this exercise to clearing out a cupboard, one I may not have looked into for a long time. Each object may have an emotional charge, but I need the space for new things; so, rather than keep everything or chucking away the lot, I need to be with each object, decide how I feel about it and either keep it or let it go.

This is a small sample of the exercises you can do to develop and maintain self-awareness. Some people might do them with a therapist or in a therapy group, but you can also do them on your own or with friends. Doing these exercises, like the job of staying sane, is an endeavour that is never finished. I have done the genogram many times and always find something new. I practise the 1234 Breathing Exercise and the Grounding Exercise as part of my daily routine. I go through phases of keeping a diary and I like to keep the expansion of my comfort zone in mind. I would not claim I feel completely sane at all times but I feel this practice helps me in my efforts to achieve this.

Notes

Introduction

1   I first read of this idea in Dan Siegel's book *Mindsight*.
2   Adapted from an idea by Louis Cozolino's *The Neuroscience of Psychotherapy*, (Norton, 2012) p.26

1. Self-Observation

3   This exercise is an adaptation from a similar exercise in Janette Rainwater's book *You're in Charge: A Guide to Becoming Your Own Therapist*, (De Vorss & Company, 2000).
4   There is further information about these experiments here: http://nobelprize.org/educational/medicine/split-brain/background.html.
5   This idea is expanded upon in Alice Miller's book *The Untouched Key: Tracing Childhood Trauma in Creativity and Destructiveness* (Virago, 1990).
6   Simon Baron-Cohen explained the possible behavioural consequences of lack of empathy in his book *Zero Degrees of Empathy: a New Theory of Human Cruelty* (Allen Lane, 2011).

7 T-cells are a particularly important part of our immune systems and they can be measured to assess our health and ability to fight diseases.

8 http://www.huffingtonpost.com/ocean-robbins/having-grati-tude-_b_1073105.html?ref=fb&src=sp&comm_ref=false

9 Julia Cameron, in her book *The Artist's Way* (Pan Books, 2011), refers to this method as 'Morning Pages'.

10 http://lapleineconscience.com/wp-content/uploads/2011/11/Holzel-etal-PPS-2011.pdf

2. Relating to Others

11 Neuroplasticity is the brain and nervous system's capacity to change structurally and functionally as a result of input from the environment. Plasticity occurs by forming new neural pathways which allow new ways of thinking, reacting, feeling and relating to become familiar as the new pathways become established.

12 Carl Rogers founded a school of humanistic counselling based on empathy rather than interpretation.

13 Spoken by a trauma consultant in the opening credits of the Channel 4 series, *24 Hours in A&E*.

14 I got this from Kate Fox's book, *Watching the English* (Hodder, 2005).

15 Kate Fox, *Watching the English*.

3. Stress

16 For more on the power of vulnerability, see this 'Ted Talk' by Brene Brown http://www.ted.com/talks/brene_brown_on_vulnerability.html.

17 This idea is from Robert M. Pirsig's *Zen and the Art of Motorcycle Maintenance* (Vintage, 1999).

18 To learn more about the different learning styles try Googling Howard Gardner; e.g: http://www.infed.org/thinkers/gardner.htm.

4. What's the Story?

19 I first read about co-constructed narratives in Louis Cozolino's *The Neuroscience of Psychotherapy*.

20 http://en.wikipedia.org/wiki/Cultivation_theory.

21 Maruta, Colligan, Malinchor & Offord, 2002; Peterson, Seligman & Vaillant, 1988. Quoted in *The Healthy Aging Brain*, Cozolino (Norton, 2008).

22 Cozolino, *The Healthy Aging Brain*.

23 I made that one up but I believe it.

24 I got this tale from *You're in Charge: A Guide to Becoming Your Own Therapist* by Janette Rainwater.

25 Someone else's faith in you when you have doubts in your ability can carry you through to success, if you allow their optimism to override your pessimism.

5. Exercises

26 This exercise is slightly adapted from one in *You're in Charge: A Guide to Becoming Your Own Therapist* by Janette Rainwater.

27 This exercise was inspired by a workshop I attended at a UKAPI conference in 2003 run by Jochen Lude.

28 If you Google 'genogram' you will be able to find software to help you make the genogram. I have not used it myself but perhaps it is useful.

Homework

A large number of books, articles and conversations contributed towards the ideas in this book. The following were particularly useful and are highly recommended not only for their inspiration and the information they contain but as good reads in themselves.

SIMON BARON-COHEN, *Zero Degrees of Empathy*
Presenting a new way of understanding what it is that leads individuals to treat others inhumanely, this book challenges us to reconsider the concept of evil.

LOUIS COZOLINO, *The Healthy Aging Brain: Sustaining Attachment, Attaining Wisdom*; *The Neuroscience of Human Relationships: Attachment and the Developing Social Brain*; *The Neuroscience of Psychotherapy: Healing the Social Brain*
Louis Cozolino is a master at synthesizing neuroscientific information to make it accessible to non-scientists. He illustrates the deep connection between our neurobiology and our social lives as well as demonstrating the practical applications of his knowledge.

NORMAN DOIDGE, *The Brain that Changes Itself*
An explanation of neuroplasticity and how our brains can repair themselves through the power of focusing and exercises.

Maria Gilbert and Vanja Orlans, *Integrative Therapy*
Explains, in depth, the workings of psychotherapy: its concepts, techniques, strategies and processes.

Alice Miller, *The Untouched Key: Tracing Childhood Trauma in Creativity and Destructiveness*
I regret that this book is currently out of print, but if you can get hold of a copy it will explain how childhood trauma can lead to either creativity or destructiveness, and the factors that make the difference.

Philippa Perry, *Couch Fiction*
This introduction to psychotherapy shows, in graphic-novel format, how therapy works and what to expect from it.

Janette Rainwater, *You're in Charge: A Guide to Becoming Your Own Therapist*
This practical self-help book offers ideas and exercises that enable the reader to act as their own therapist.

Daniel Siegel, *Mindsight*
Contemplative practice can be used for sustaining good mental health and to alleviate a range of psychological and interpersonal problems. This book explains how, and offers case studies.

David Snowdon, *Aging with Grace*
This book shows us that old age does not have to mean an inevitable slide into illness and disability; rather, it can be a time of promise and productivity, of intellectual vigour and freedom from disease.

Acknowledgements

I'd like to thank Alain de Botton for his faith in me that I could write a self-help book and for continuing that faith when I was short of it myself. I am grateful to various readers for their encouragement and feedback: Julianne Appel-Opper, Dorothy Charles, Lynn Keane, Nicola Blunden, Daisy Goodwin, Stuart Paterson, Galit Ferguson, Jane Phillimore and Morgwn Rimel.

I'd like to thank the Pan Macmillan team, Liz Gough, Tania Adams and Will Atkins for their editing skills. Thank you to Marcia Mihotich for her illustrations and for being a pleasure to work with. I am grateful to Gillian Holding for a useful anecdote. I am very much indebted to Stella Tillyard for all her reading of various stages of the manuscript and her belief, encouragement, friendship and practical help. Any errors in this work are all mine. I am deeply grateful to my loving husband Grayson and daughter Flo who help to keep me sane, every day.

Notes

Notes

If you enjoyed this book and want to read more about life's big issues, you can find out about the series, buy books and get access to exclusive content at www.panmacmillan.com/theschooloflife

If you'd like to explore ideas for everyday living, THE SCHOOL OF LIFE runs a regular programme of classes, weekends, secular sermons and events in London and other cities around the world. Browse our shop and visit www.theschooloflife.com

**How to Thrive
in the Digital Age**
Tom Chatfield

**How to Think
More about Sex**
Alain de Botton

**How to Change
the World**
John-Paul Flintoff

**How to Worry
Less about Money**
John Armstrong

**How to
Stay Sane**
Philippa Perry

**How to Find
Fulfilling Work**
Roman Krznaric